THE PRESIDENTS:

Washington to Reagan

Ottenheimer Publishers, Inc.
Baltimore, Maryland 21208

The Artist

Not surprisingly, Mr. Sam J. Patrick was born not too far from the Liberty Bell in Philadelphia in 1908. Gifted with a natural talent for drawing, he chose an early career for himself in the world of art. As a youth, he studied art in night classes at the Spring Garden Institute while working in the steel mills and the Philadelphia Navy Yard. Motivated by a compelling spirit of adventure and curiosity, he traveled across the country to California where he continued his studies at the Otis Art Institute. A fresh, exciting portfolio gained him a position in the art department of a Los Angeles newspaper. This was to be the beginning of a rewarding 40 year career as a top newspaper staff artist.

Mr. Patrick's exceptional skill as an illustrator has enabled him to collaborate with many writers and authors in the creation of internationally syndicated features. His work has appeared in more than 600 newspapers throughout the world.

These portraits represent the culmination of years of dedicated experimentation and development to refine a new technique and a new medium. Mr. Patrick can truly be called "the master" of this new technique. Essentially, it entails the use of special wax colored pencils which impart a remarkable realism and detail to the color portrait.

In Mr. Patrick's words, "the portraits were designed to rekindle pride in those distinguished men who overcame adversity in themselves and in the nation." His noble endeavor has obviously been achieved, for among his many citations and awards he can take particular pride in winning the coveted George Washington Honor Medal from the Freedoms Foundation at Valley Forge.

Manufactured in Hong Kong

ISBN: 0-517-433508

h   g   f   e   d   c   b   a

Contents

Introduction

Article II, Section 1 of the Constitution of the United States provides:
"The Executive power shall be vested in a President of the United States of America. He shall hold his office during the term of four years, and together with the Vice President, chosen for the same term, be elected. . ."

Presidential Qualifications

In order to become a candidate for the presidency, said candidate must be a natural born citizen of the United States. The minimum age for a candidate is 35 years, and residence in the United States must be established for at least 14 years.

Presidential Powers and Duties

The duly-elected President of the United States is also the Commander-in-Chief of the Armed Forces. He receives representatives of foreign governments and devises treaties with the advice and consent of the Senate. The President communicates with Congress by message and has the power to approve or veto Congressional acts. He can also call and adjourn special sessions of Congress.

In addition, the President appoints public officers with the Senate's approval. He is also able to grant reprieves and pardons for crimes committed against the United States.

The Process of Election

The framers of the Constitution did not allow for direct, popular election of the President and Vice President. Instead, they established the *Electoral College* — consisting of state electors chosen at a general election. The number of electors chosen is equal to the state's number of senators and representatives in Congress. A majority of electoral votes is required in order for a president to be elected.

A general election is held nation-wide on the Tuesday following the first Monday of November of every fourth year. This date was fixed by an act of Congress in 1845. The electors of the political party receiving the highest vote become the ones to cast a ballot for the Presidential office.

December 15, following the election, the electors meet in their own states and vote by ballot for the President and Vice President. These votes are then sent to the President of the Senate.

Before both houses of Congress, the President of the Senate opens and reads the ballots aloud on January 6. If there is a clear majority, the newly-elected President and Vice President are announced.

In the event that there is no choice by the state electors, the House of Representatives elects the President by voting between the three candidates that received the highest electoral votes. All state representatives combine to cast one vote. If the Vice Presidency does not command a majority, that vote goes into the Senate, where the Senators vote individually between the top two names.

George Washington

(1732 - 1799) First President

BORN	February 22, 1732
PLACE OF BIRTH	Pope's Creek, Westmoreland County, Virginia
ANCESTRY	English
FATHER	Augustine Washington (1694 - 1743)
MOTHER	Mary Ball Washington (1708 - 1789)
WIFE	Martha Dandridge Custis (1731 - 1802)
CHILDREN	None (adopted two children from his wife's first marriage)
EDUCATION	Private tutors
RELIGION	Episcopalian
OCCUPATION	Surveyor, soldier, planter
MILITARY SERVICE	Virginia Militia (1752-1758); Commander in Chief of 1st Continental Army (1775-1783)
POLITICAL PARTY	Federalist
OFFICES HELD	Member, Virginia House of Burgesses; Justice of Fairfax County; President of Constitutional Convention
AGE AT INAUGURATION	57
TERMS SERVED	Two (1789-1793) (1793-1797)
VICE PRESIDENT	John Adams (both terms)
DIED	December 14, 1799, Mount Vernon, Virginia, age 67
CAUSE OF DEATH	Pneumonia

HIGHLIGHTS OF HISTORICAL EVENTS DURING WASHINGTON'S ADMINISTRATION (1789-1797) (U.S. Poplulation 3,929,214)

POLITICAL	1789	Washington elected first President of U.S.; first Congress meets; Supreme Court and Cabinet established
	1790	Capital temporarily moved from New York to Philadelphia; first U.S. Census
	1791	Bill of Rights becomes part of U.S. Constitution; Bank of U.S. established; District of Columbia formed
	1792	Congress establishes U.S. Mint; Presidential Succession Act
	1793	Washington's Neutrality Proclamation; Jefferson resigns as Secretary of State; Citizen Genet affair
	1794	Jay's Treaty signed in London; Whisky Rebellion put down; 11th Amendment proposed in Congress
	1795	Washington reorganizes the Cabinet; Pinckney's Treaty signed in Madrid
	1796	Washington gives his farewell address; John Adams elected President
MILITARY	1789	Department of War established
SCIENTIFIC	1792	Gas lighting - William Murdock, Scotland
	1793	Cotton gin - Eli Whitney, U.S.
TERRITORY		States admitted: Vermont, 1791; Kentucky, 1792; Tennessee, 1796

John Adams

(1735 - 1826) Second President

BORN	October 19, 1735
PLACE OF BIRTH	Braintree (Quincy), Massachusetts
ANCESTRY	English
FATHER	John Adams (1691 - 1761)
MOTHER	Susanna Boylston Adams (1699 - 1797)
WIFE	Abigail Smith (1744 - 1818)
CHILDREN	Five: 3 boys, 2 girls
EDUCATION	Private schools; received B.A. (1755) and M.A. (1758) from Harvard
RELIGION	Unitarian
OCCUPATION	Teacher, farmer, lawyer
MILITARY SERVICE	None
POLITICAL PARTY	Federalist
OFFICES HELD	Representative to Massachusetts General Court; Delegate to First and Second Continental Congresses; Member of Provincial Congress of Massachusetts; Delegate to Massachusetts Constitutional Convention; Commissioner to France; Minister to Netherlands and England; Vice President
AGE AT INAUGURATION	61
TERMS SERVED	One (1797 - 1801)
VICE PRESIDENT	Thomas Jefferson
DIED	July 4, 1826, Quincy, Massachusetts, age 90
CAUSE OF DEATH	Natural causes

HIGHLIGHTS OF HISTORICAL EVENTS DURING ADAMS' ADMINISTRATION (1797 - 1801) (U.S. Population 4,883,209)

POLITICAL	1798	XYZ Affair; Alien and Sedition Act
	1799	Fries Uprising, death of Washington
	1800	Treaty of Morfontaine; Adams loses election; Washington, D.C. becomes nation's capital
	1801	John Marshall appointed Chief Justice; Jefferson inaugurated
MILITARY	1798	Navy Department created; Washington appointed Commander of Provisional Army
SCIENTIFIC	1800	Electric battery - Alessandro Volta, Italy
TERRITORY	No states admitted	

12

Thomas Jefferson

(1743 - 1826) Third President

BORN	April 13, 1743
PLACE OF BIRTH	Shadwell, Albemarle County, Virginia
ANCESTRY	Welsh
FATHER	Peter Jefferson (1708 - 1757)
MOTHER	Jane Randolph Jefferson (1720 - 1776)
WIFE	Martha Wayles Skelton (Patty) (1748 - 1782)
CHILDREN	Six: 1 boy, 5 girls (2 girls and the boy died in infancy)
EDUCATION	Private tutoring; country school in Albemarle; B.A. (1762) from College of William and Mary
RELIGION	No formal affiliation
OCCUPATION	Lawyer, inventor, author
MILITARY SERVICE	Colonel of County Militia, Virginia
POLITICAL PARTY	Democratic-Republican
OFFICES HELD	Member of Virginia House of Burgesses; County Lieutenant; County Surveyor; Deputy Delegate to Second Continental Congress; Member of Virginia House of Delegates; Governor of Virginia; Commissioner to France; Minister to France; Secretary of State; Vice President
AGE AT INAUGURATION	57
TERMS SERVED	Two (1801 - 1805) (1805 - 1809)
VICE PRESIDENTS	Aaron Burr (1801 - 1805) and George Clinton (1805 - 1809)
DIED	July 4, 1826, "Monticello," Charlottesville, Virginia, age 83
CAUSE OF DEATH	Natural causes

HIGHLIGHTS OF HISTORICAL EVENTS DURING JEFFERSON'S ADMINISTRATION (1801 - 1809) (U.S. Population 5,485,528)

POLITICAL	1801	Judiciary Act
	1802	Judiciary Act and Excise Tax repealed
	1803	Marbury vs. Madison; Louisiana Purchase
	1804	Burr and Hamilton duel; Jefferson re-elected; Napoleon becomes Emperor of France; Lewis and Clark Expedition
	1807	Aaron Burr conspiracy and trial; Chesapeake and Leonard affair; Embargo Act
	1808	Abolishment of slave trade; first national highway construction authorized
MILITARY	1801	Tripoli declares war on U.S.
	1802	Congress makes West Point first U.S. Military Academy
SCIENTIFIC	1804	Locomotive - Richard Trevithick, England
	1807	Steamship - Robert Fulton, U.S.
TERRITORY		State admitted: Ohio, 1803

James Madison

(1751 - 1836) Fourth President

BORN	March 16, 1751
PLACE OF BIRTH	Port Conway, Virginia
ANCESTRY	English
FATHER	James Madison (1723 - 1801)
MOTHER	Eleanor Conway Monroe (1732 - 1829)
WIFE	Dorothea (Dolley) Payne Todd (1768 - 1819)
CHILDREN	None
EDUCATION	Early education at Donald Robertson's School and from private tutor; awarded A.B. (1771) from College of New Jersey (Princeton); one year postgraduate study at Princeton
RELIGION	Episcopalian
OCCUPATION	Lawyer, author
MILITARY SERVICE	None
POLITICAL PARTY	Democratic-Republican
OFFICES HELD	Member of Orange County Committee of Safety; Delegate to the Virginia Convention; Member of Virginia Legislature; Member of Virginia Executive Council; Delegate to Continental Congress; Delegate to Annapolis Convention; Delegate to Constitutional Convention; Member of Virginia Ratification Convention; U.S. Congressman; Secretary of State
AGE AT INAUGURATION	57
TERMS SERVED	Two (1809 - 1813) (1813 - 1817)
VICE PRESIDENTS	George Clinton (1809 - 1812, died in office) and Elbridge Gerry (1813 - 1814, died in office)
DIED	June 28, 1836, Montpelier, Virginia, age 85
CAUSE OF DEATH	Natural causes

HIGHLIGHTS OF HISTORICAL EVENTS DURING MADISON'S ADMINISTRATION (1809 - 1817) (U.S. Population 7,030,647)

POLITICAL	1810	Macon Bill No. 2; West Florida annexed
	1812	**Hostilities with Britain; British blockade**
	1814	British burn Washington, D.C.; Treaty of Ghent ends War of 1812; Hartford Convention
	1816	Second U.S. Bank created; Monroe elected President
MILITARY	1811	General Harrison defeats Tecumseh at Tippecanoe
	1812	U.S. battles Britain
	1813	Creek War
	1815	Battle of New Orleans; establishment of Peacetime Army
SCIENTIFIC	1816	**Miner's safety lamp - Humphry Davy, English**
TERRITORY		States admitted: Louisiana, 1812; Indiana, 1816

James Monroe

(1758 - 1831) Fifth President

BORN	April 28, 1758
PLACE OF BIRTH	Westmoreland County, Virginia
ANCESTRY	Scotch
FATHER	Spence Monroe (? - 1774)
MOTHER	Elizabeth Jones Monroe (? - ?)
WIFE	Elizabeth Kortright (1768 - 1830)
CHILDREN	Two girls
EDUCATION	Parson Campbell School; College of William and Mary
RELIGION	Episcopalian
OCCUPATION	Lawyer, senator, diplomat
MILITARY SERVICE	Officer in Third Virginia Regiment and Continental Army (1776 - 1779)
POLITICAL PARTY	Democratic-Republican
OFFICES HELD	Military Commissioner for Southern Army; Representative to Virginia Legislature; Member of Governor Jefferson's Council; Representative to Virginia House of Delegates; Representative to Continental Congress; Representative to Virginia Assembly; Representative to U.S. Senate; Minister to France; Minister to England; Governor of Virginia; Secretary of State; Secretary of War
AGE AT INAUGURATION	58
TERMS SERVED	Two (1817 - 1821) (1821 - 1825)
VICE PRESIDENT	Daniel D. Tompkins (both terms)
DIED	July 4, 1831, New York, New York, age 73
CAUSE OF DEATH	Natural causes

HIGHLIGHTS OF HISTORICAL EVENTS DURING MONROE'S ADMINISTRATION (1817 - 1825) (U.S. Population 8,898,892)

POLITICAL	1817	Construction of Erie Canal starts
	1818	Convention of 1818, signed in London
	1819	Financial panic seizes nation; Spain concedes East Florida to U.S.
	1820	Missouri Compromise
	1823	Monroe Doctrine proclaimed
	1824	John Quincy Adams elected President without a majority; House chooses Adams
MILITARY	1818	First Seminole Wars
SCIENTIFIC	1822	Electric Motor - Michael Faraday, England

TERRITORY   States admitted: Mississippi, 1817; Illinois, 1818; Alabama, 1819; Maine, 1820; Missouri, 1821

John Q. Adams

(1767 - 1848) Sixth President

BORN	July 11, 1767
PLACE OF BIRTH	Braintree (Quincy), Massachusetts
ANCESTRY	English
FATHER	John Adams (1735-1826)
MOTHER	Abigail Smith Adams (1744-1818)
WIFE	Louisa Catherine Johnson (1775 - 1852)
CHILDREN	Four: 3 boys, 1 girl
EDUCATION	Studied in Paris, Amsterdam, Leiden and The Hague; B.A. (1787) from Harvard; studied law (1788 - 1790) with Theophilus Parsons
RELIGION	Unitarian
OCCUPATION	Lawyer; professor
MILITARY SERVICE	None
POLITICAL PARTY	Federalist, 1808; Democrat-Republican to 1825; National Republican thereafter
OFFICES HELD	Minister to the Netherlands; Minister to Prussia; Member of Massachusetts Senate; Member of U.S. Senate; Minister to Russia; Minister to Great Britain; Secretary of State
AGE AT INAUGURATION	57
TERMS SERVED	One (1825-1829)
VICE PRESIDENT	John C. Calhoun
DIED	February 23, 1848, Washington, D.C., age 80
CAUSE OF DEATH	Stroke

HIGHLIGHTS OF HISTORICAL EVENTS DURING ADAMS' ADMINISTRATION (1825 - 1829) (U.S. Population 11,252,237)

POLITICAL	1825	Civil Service policy; Democrats and Republicans split into separate parties
	1826	Panama Congress; death of Thomas Jefferson and John Adams
	1828	Tariff of Abominations
	1829	Construction starts on Baltimore and Ohio Railroad
SCIENTIFIC	1828	Blast furnace - J.B. Neilson, Scotland
TERRITORY	No states admitted	

Andrew Jackson

(1767 - 1845) Seventh President

BORN	March 15, 1767
PLACE OF BIRTH	The Waxhaws, South Carolina
ANCESTRY	Scotch Irish
FATHER	Andrew Jackson (? - 1767)
MOTHER	Elizabeth Hutchinson Jackson (? - 1781)
WIFE	Rachel Donelson Robards (1767 - 1828)
CHILDREN	One boy (adopted)
EDUCATION	Attended public schools; studied law in Salisbury, South Carolina
RELIGION	Presbyterian
OCCUPATION	Lawyer, soldier, congressman
MILITARY SERVICE	Judge advocate of Davidson County Militia (c. 1791); Major General of Tennessee Militia (1802 - 1812); Major General of U.S. Army (1814 - 1821)
POLITICAL PARTY	Democrat
OFFICES HELD	Attorney General of Western District of North Carolina; Delegate to Tennessee State Constitutional Convention; Member of U.S. House of Representatives; Member of U.S. Senate; Tennessee Supreme Court Judge; Governor of Florida Territory
AGE AT INAUGURATION	61
TERMS SERVED	Two (1829 - 1833) (1833 - 1837)
VICE PRESIDENTS	John C. Calhoun (1829 - 1832, resigned) and Martin Van Buren (1833 - 1837)
DIED	June 8, 1845, Nashville, Tennessee, age 78
CAUSE OF DEATH	Natural causes

HIGHLIGHTS OF HISTORICAL EVENTS DURING JACKSON'S ADMINISTRATION (1829 - 1837) (U.S. Population 12,565,145)

POLITICAL	1829	Jackson's Kitchen Cabinet
	1830	Webster-Hayne debates; Maysville Road veto; Oregon Trail
	1831	Jackson breaks with Calhoun; Cabinet reorganized
	1832	U.S. Bank Recharter Bill vetoed; tariff laws nullified
	1833	Deposits removed from Bank of U.S.; Abolitionist Movement attracts national attention
	1834	Whig Party formed
	1835	Jackson narrowly escapes assassination
	1836	Texas declares independence; Siege of the Alamo
MILITARY	1832	Black Hawk War
	1835	Second Seminole War
SCIENTIFIC	1832	Electric telegraph - Samuel Morse, U.S.
	1834	Reaping machine - Cyrus McCormick, U.S.
	1835	Revolver - Samuel Colt, U.S.
TERRITORY		States admitted: Arkansas, 1836; Michigan, 1837

Martin Van Buren

(1782 - 1862) Eighth President

BORN	December 5, 1782
PLACE OF BIRTH	Kinderhook, New York
ANCESTRY	Dutch
FATHER	Abraham Van Buren (1737 - 1817)
MOTHER	Maria Hoes Van Alen Van Buren (1747 - 1817)
WIFE	Hannah Hoes (1783 - 1819)
CHILDREN	Four boys
EDUCATION	Village schools; studied in law office
RELIGION	Dutch Reformed
OCCUPATION	Lawyer, senator
MILITARY SERVICE	None
POLITICAL PARTY	Democrat during Presidency (Free-Soil from 1848)
OFFICES HELD	Surrogate of Columbia County, New York; New York State Senator; Attorney General of New York; Delegate to Third New York State Constitutional Convention; U.S. Senator; Governor of New York; Secretary of State; Vice President
AGE AT INAUGURATION	54
TERMS SERVED	One (1837 - 1841)
VICE PRESIDENT	Richard M. Johnson
DIED	July 24, 1862, Kinderhook, New York, age 79
CAUSE OF DEATH	Natural causes

HIGHLIGHTS OF HISTORICAL EVENTS DURING VAN BUREN'S ADMINISTRATION (1837 - 1841) (U.S. Population 15,843,452)

POLITICAL	1837	Bank panic and depression
	1838	Caroline Affair
	1839	Ten-hour work day established; Liberty Party formed
	1840	Underground railroad organized; Independent Treasury Act; Harrison elected President
MILITARY	1838	Aroostook War
SCIENTIFIC	1839	Vulcanized rubber - Charles Goodyear, U.S.
	1839	On paper photography - William Fox-Talbot, England
TERRITORY		No states admitted

William H. Harrison

(1773 - 1841) Ninth President

BORN	February 9, 1773
PLACE OF BIRTH	Berkley (Charles City County), Virginia
ANCESTRY	English
FATHER	Benjamin Harrison (1726 - 1791)
MOTHER	Elizabeth Bassett Harrison (1730 - 1792)
WIFE	Anna Tuthill Symmes (1775 - 1864)
CHILDREN	Ten: 6 boys, 4 girls
EDUCATION	Private tutoring; attended Hampden-Sidney College
RELIGION	Episcopalian
OCCUPATION	Soldier, congressman, governor
MILITARY SERVICE	U.S. Army (1791 - 1798), rose from Ensign to Captain; as Governor of Indiana Territory, fought Indians at Tippecanoe (1811); commissioned Major General of Kentucky Militia (1812); U.S. Army (1812 - 1814), rose from Brigadier General to Major General in command of the Northwest
POLITICAL PARTY	Whig
OFFICES HELD	Secretary of Northwest Territory; U.S. Representative; Governor of Indiana Territory and Superintendent of Indian Affairs; Ohio State Senator; U.S. Senator; Minister to Colombia
AGE AT INAUGURATION	68
TERMS SERVED	One (one month, died in office 1841)
VICE PRESIDENT	John Tyler
DIED	April 4, 1841, Washington, D.C., age 68
CAUSE OF DEATH	Pneumonia

HIGHLIGHTS OF HISTORICAL EVENTS DURING HARRISON'S ADMINISTRATION (1841 - 1841) (U.S. Population 17,732,715)

POLITICAL	1841	Repeal of Independent Treasury Act; Harrison dies after serving one month in office; Tyler elected President
TERRITORY	No states admitted	

John Tyler

(1790 - 1862) Tenth President

BORN	March 29, 1790
PLACE OF BIRTH	Greenway (Charles City County), Virginia
ANCESTRY	English
FATHER	John Tyler (1747-1813)
MOTHER	Mary Marot Armistead Tyler (1761-1797)
WIVES	First Wife: Letitia Christian (1790-1842)
	Second Wife: Julia Gardiner (1820-1889)
CHILDREN	First wife: Seven - 3 boys, 4 girls
	Second wife: Seven - 5 boys, 2 girls
EDUCATION	Local Virginia Schools; graduated from College of William and Mary (1807)
RELIGION	Episcopalian
OCCUPATION	Lawyer, governor
MILITARY SERVICE	Captain of Volunteer Company in Richmond, Virginia (1813)
POLITICAL PARTY	Whig
OFFICES HELD	Member of Virginia House of Delegates; U.S. Representative; Governor of Virginia; U.S. Senator, Vice President
AGE AT INAUGURATION	51
TERMS SERVED	One (1841-1845)
VICE PRESIDENT	None
DIED	January 18, 1862, Richmond, Virginia, age 71
CAUSE OF DEATH	Illness due to bronchitis

HIGHLIGHTS OF HISTORICAL EVENTS DURING TYLER'S ADMINISTRATION (1841 - 1845) (U.S. Population 17,732,715)

POLITICAL	1841	Cabinet resigns; Dorr Rebellion
	1842	Webster-Ashburton Treaty
	1844	Oregon debate; Polk elected to office
	1845	Annexation of Texas
SCIENTIFIC	1845	Double-tube tire - Robert W. Thompson, England
TERRITORY		States admitted: Florida, 1845

James K. Polk

(1795 - 1849) Eleventh President

BORN	November 2, 1795
PLACE OF BIRTH	Mecklenburg County, North Carolina
ANCESTRY	Scotch-Irish
FATHER	Samuel Polk (1772 - 1827)
MOTHER	Jane Knox Polk (1776 - 1852)
WIFE	Sarah Childress (1803 - 1891)
CHILDREN	None
EDUCATION	Private school; B.A. from University of North Carolina
RELIGION	Presbyterian
OCCUPATION	Lawyer
MILITARY SERVICE	None
POLITICAL PARTY	Democrat
OFFICES HELD	Member of Tennessee Legislature; U.S. Representative; Speaker of House of Representatives; Governor of Tennessee
AGE AT INAUGURATION	49
TERMS SERVED	One (1845 - 1849)
VICE PRESIDENT	George M. Dallas
DIED	June 15, 1849, Nashville, Tennessee, age 53
CAUSE OF DEATH	Heart failure

HIGHLIGHTS OF HISTORICAL EVENTS DURING POLK'S ADMINISTRATION (1845 - 1849) (U.S. Population 20,181,683)

POLITICAL	1845	Boundary disputes with Mexico; Slidell Mission to Mexico
	1846	Oregon settlement; Wilmot Proviso; acquisition of California
	1847	Brigham Young settles Mormon's at Salt Lake City, Utah
	1848	Gold discovered in California
MILITARY	1845	U.S. Naval Academy established at Annapolis
	1846	U.S. declares war on Mexico; Battle of Palo Alto
	1847	Battle of Buena Vista; capture of Veracruz
SCIENTIFIC	1846	Sewing machine - Elias Howe, U.S.
	1846	Rotary printing press - Richard Hoe, U.S.
TERRITORY		States admitted: Texas, 1845; Iowa, 1846; Wisconsin, 1848

Zachary Taylor

(1784 - 1850) Twelfth President

BORN	November 24, 1784
PLACE OF BIRTH	Orange County, Virginia
ANCESTRY	English
FATHER	Lieutenant Colonel Richard Taylor (1744 - 1829)
MOTHER	Sarah Dabney Strother Taylor (1760 - 1822)
WIFE	Margaret Mackall Smith (1788 - 1852)
CHILDREN	Six; 1 boy, 5 girls
EDUCATION	Private tutors
RELIGION	Episcopalian
OCCUPATION	Soldier, farmer
MILITARY SERVICE	Volunteer in Kentucky Militia (1803); rose from First Lieutenant to Major General in U.S. Army (1808 - 1849)
POLITICAL PARTY	Whig
OFFICES HELD	None
AGE AT INAUGURATION	64
TERMS SERVED	One (1849 - 1850, died in office)
VICE PRESIDENT	Millard Fillmore
DIED	July 9, 1850, Washington, D.C., age 65
CAUSE OF DEATH	Cholera

HIGHLIGHTS OF HISTORICAL EVENTS DURING TAYLOR'S ADMINISTRATION (1849 - 1850) (U.S. Population 22,630,654)

POLITICAL	1850	Fugitive Slave Act; Clayton Bulwer Treaty; Hawaiian Islands Treaty; Nashville Convention; Taylor dies in office July 9
SCIENTIFIC	1849	Safety pin - Walter Hunt, U.S.
TERRITORY	No states admitted	

Millard Fillmore

(1800 - 1874) Thirteenth President

BORN	January 7, 1800
PLACE OF BIRTH	Locke (Cayuga County) New York
ANCESTRY	English
FATHER	Nathaniel Fillmore (1771 - 1863)
MOTHER	Phoebe Millard Fillmore (1780 - 1831)
WIVES	First wife: Abigail Powers (1771 - 1853)
	Second wife: Caroline Carmichael McIntosh (1813 - 1881)
CHILDREN	Two: one boy, one girl (by first wife)
EDUCATION	Attended public schools; studied law in Cayuga County and Buffalo, New York
RELIGION	Unitarian
OCCUPATION	Lawyer, teacher, congressman
MILITARY SERVICE	None
POLITICAL PARTY	Whig
OFFICES HELD	Member of New York Legislature; Member of U.S. House of Representatives; Vice President
AGE AT INAUGURATION	50
TERMS SERVED	One (1850 - 1853)
VICE PRESIDENT	None
DIED	March 8, 1874, Buffalo, New York, age 74
CAUSE OF DEATH	Stroke

HIGHLIGHTS OF HISTORICAL EVENTS DURING FILLMORE'S ADMINISTRATION (1850 - 1853) (U.S. Population 23,260,638)

POLITICAL	1850	Clay's Resolutions (Compromise Act of 1950); Fugitive Slave Law enforced
	1851	French attempt to annex Hawaii
	1852	Fillmore loses Whig support for nomination; Harriet Beecher Stowe's "Uncle Tom's Cabin" published
SCIENTIFIC	1851	Refrigerating machine - John Gorrie, U.S.
	1852	Electric elevator - Elisha G. Otis, U.S.
TERRITORY		State admitted: California, 1850

Franklin Pierce

(1804 - 1869) Fourteenth President

BORN	November 23, 1804
PLACE OF BIRTH	Hillsboro, New Hampshire
ANCESTRY	English
FATHER	Benjamin Pierce (1757 - 1839)
MOTHER	Anna Kendrick Pierce (1768 - 1838)
WIFE	Jane Means Appleton (1806 - 1863)
CHILDREN	Two boys
EDUCATION	Attended public school and Hancock Academy; graduated from Bowdoin College (1824)
RELIGION	Episcopalian
OCCUPATION	Lawyer, soldier
MILITARY SERVICE	Brigadier General in U.S. Army (1847 - 1848)
POLITICAL PARTY	Democrat
OFFICES HELD	Member and Speaker of New Hampshire Legislature; Member of U.S. House of Representatives; Member of Senate; President of New Hampshire Constitutional Convention
AGE AT INAUGURATION	48
TERMS SERVED	One (1853 - 1857)
VICE PRESIDENT	William R. King
DIED	October 8, 1869, Concord, New Hampshire, age 64
CAUSE OF DEATH	Natural causes

HIGHLIGHTS OF HISTORICAL EVENTS DURING PIERCE'S ADMINISTRATION (1853 - 1857) (U.S. Population 25,736,070)

POLITICAL	1853	Gadsdeon Purchase; Commodore Perry opens trade with Japan
	1854	Kansas-Nebraska Act; Canadian Reciprocity Treaty; Republican Party formed; Ostend Manifesto
	1856	Violent civil war in Kansas
MILITARY	1855	Walker's invasion of Nicaragua
SCIENTIFIC	1855	Steel production - Henry Bessemer, England
TERRITORY	No states admitted	

James Buchanan

(1791 - 1868) Fifteenth President

BORN	April 23, 1791
PLACE OF BIRTH	Cove Gap, Pennsylvania
ANCESTRY	Scotch-Irish
FATHER	James Buchanan (1761 - 1821)
MOTHER	Elizabeth Speer Buchanan (1767 - 1833)
WIFE	None (not married)
CHILDREN	None
EDUCATION	Attended Old Stone Academy; graduated from Dickinson College (1809)
RELIGION	Presbyterian
OCCUPATION	Lawyer, author
MILITARY SERVICE	None
POLITICAL PARTY	Democrat
OFFICES HELD	Member of Pennsylvania Legislature; Member of U.S. House of Representatives; Minister to Russia; Member of U.S. Senate; Secretary of State; Minister to Great Britain
AGE AT INAUGURATION	65
TERMS SERVED	One (1857 - 1861)
VICE PRESIDENT	John C. Breckinridge
DIED	June 1, 1868, Lancaster, Pennsylvania, age 77
CAUSE OF DEATH	Natural causes

HIGHLIGHTS OF HISTORICAL EVENTS DURING BUCHANAN'S ADMINISTRATION (1857 - 1861) (U.S. Population 29,036,649)

POLITICAL	1857	Dred Scott decision; Missouri Compromise declared unconstitutional; Lecompton Constitution
	1858	Lincoln-Douglas debates; completion of Atlantic Cable
	1859	John Brown's Raid at Harper's Ferry
	1860	South Carolina secedes from Union; Pony Express mail service
	1861	Confederacy formed by 11 seceding states; Southern Provisional Government established; Lincoln inaugurated
MILITARY	1861	Southern states form separate militia
SCIENTIFIC	1860	Repeating rifle - O.F. Winchester, U.S.
	1861	Machine gun - Richard J. Gatling, U.S.
TERRITORY		States admitted: Minnesota, 1858; Oregon, 1859; Kansas, 1861

Abraham Lincoln

(1809 - 1865) Sixteenth President

BORN	February 12, 1809
PLACE OF BIRTH	Hardin County, Kentucky
ANCESTRY	English
FATHER	Thomas Lincoln (1778 - 1851)
MOTHER	Nancy Hanks Lincoln (1784 - 1818)
STEPMOTHER	Sarah Bush Johnston Lincoln (1788 - 1869)
WIFE	Mary Todd (1818 - 1882)
CHILDREN	Four boys
EDUCATION	Local tutors; self-educated
RELIGION	No formal affiliation
OCCUPATION	Merchant, lawyer
MILITARY SERVICE	Served in Volunteer Company for 3 months during Black Hawk War (1832)
POLITICAL PARTY	Republican
OFFICES HELD	Member of Illinois General Assembly; Member of U.S. House of Representatives
AGE OF INAUGURATION	52
TERMS SERVED	Two (1861 - 1865) (1865, died in office)
VICE PRESIDENTS	Hannibal Hamlin (1861 - 1865) and Andrew Johnson (1865)
DIED	April 15, 1865, Washington, D.C., age 56
CAUSE OF DEATH	Assassinated

HIGHLIGHTS OF HISTORICAL EVENTS DURING LINCOLN'S ADMINISTRATION (1861 - 1865) (U.S. Population 32,350,627)

POLITICAL	1861	Fort Sumter fired upon; Confederacy joined by Virginia, Arkansas, North Carolina, and Tennessee; Civil War starts; Jefferson Davis elected President of Confederacy
	1862	Morrill land-grant
	1863	Lincoln issues Emancipation Proclamation; Lincoln's Gettysburg Address; College Act; Thanksgiving declared national holiday
	1864	Lincoln re-elected
	1865	Lincoln assassinated April 14th; Andrew Johnson takes office
MILITARY	1861	General Robert E. Lee appointed Commander of Confederate Forces
	1862	Monitor vs. Merrimack; Battle of Shiloh; Second Bull Run; Battle of Antietam; Battle of Fredricksburg
	1863	National Conscription Act; Vicksburg Campaign; Lee defeated at Gettysburg
	1864	General Ulysses S. Grant becomes Commander of Union Armies; Sherman's March through Georgia
	1865	Lee surrenders at Appomattox - Civil War ends
TERRITORY		States admitted: West Virginia, 1863; Nevada, 1864

Andrew Johnson

(1808 - 1875) Seventeenth President

BORN   December 29, 1808
PLACE OF BIRTH   Raleigh, North Carolina
ANCESTRY   Scotch-Irish, English
FATHER   Jacob Johnson (? - 1812)
MOTHER   Mary McDonough Johnson (? - 1856)
WIFE   Eliza McCardle (1800 - 1876)
CHILDREN   Five: 3 boys, 2 girls
EDUCATION   Self-taught
RELIGION   No formal affiliation
OCCUPATION   Tailor
MILITARY SERVICE   None
POLITICAL PARTY   Democrat; elected Vice President on National Union Ticket
OFFICES HELD   Alderman; Mayor; Member of Tennessee Legislature; Member of U.S. House of Representatives; Governor of Tennessee; Member of U.S. Senate; Vice President
AGE AT INAUGURATION   56
TERMS SERVED   One (1865 - 1869)
VICE PRESIDENT   None
DIED   July 31, 1875, Carter County, Tennessee, age 66
CAUSE OF DEATH   Stroke

HIGHLIGHTS OF HISTORICAL EVENTS DURING JOHNSON'S ADMINISTRATION (1865 - 1869) (U.S.Population 35,700,678)

POLITICAL   1865   13th Amendment abolishes slavery; Reconstruction period; proclamation of amnesty for South
               1886   KKK organized
               1867   Johnson's reconstruction program opposed but passed over veto
               1868   Civil Rights Act gives Negroes citizenship (14th Amendment); Johnson impeached by House of Representatives, acquitted by Senate; Grant elected President; Alaska purchased for $7,200,000

MILITARY   1866   U.S. Troops ordered to Mexican Border

SCIENTIFIC   1866   Dynamite - Alfred B. Nobel, Sweden
               1867   Commercial typewriter - Christopher L. Sholes, U.S.

TERRITORY   State admitted: Nebraska, 1867

Ulysses S. Grant

(1822 - 1885) Eighteenth President

BORN	April 27, 1822
PLACE OF BIRTH	Point Pleasant, Ohio
ANCESTRY	English-Scotch
FATHER	Jesse Root Grant (1794 - 1873)
MOTHER	Hannah Simpson Grant (1798 - 1883)
WIFE	Julia Boggs Dent (1826 - 1902)
CHILDREN	Four: 3 boys, 1 girl
EDUCATION	Local schools; U.S. Military Academy
RELIGION	Methodist
OCCUPATION	Soldier, farmer, real-estate agent, Customs House clerk, leather store clerk
MILITARY SERVICE	Commissioned Second Lieutenant in 4th U.S. Infantry (1843), resigned as Captain (1854); re-entered Army in August 1861 as Brigadier General; became General in Chief of Union Armies on March 12, 1864
POLITICAL PARTY	Republican
OFFICE HELD	Secretary of War
AGE AT INAUGURATION	46
TERMS SERVED	Two (1869 - 1873) (1873 - 1877)
VICE PRESIDENTS	Schuyler Colfax (1869 - 1873) and Henry Wilson (1873 - 1875, died in office)
DIED	July 23, 1885, Mt. McGregor, New York, age 63
CAUSE OF DEATH	Throat cancer

HIGHLIGHTS OF HISTORICAL EVENTS DURING GRANT'S ADMINISTRATION (1869 - 1877) (U.S. Population 39,050,729)

POLITICAL	1869	Gould-Fisk scandal; "Black Friday"; transcontinental railroad completed
	1870	Negroes given right to vote (15th Amendment ratified)
	1871	Department of Justice created; Civil Service reform
	1872	Administrative scandals (Credit Mobilier)
	1873	Financial panic and 5-year depression; "Salary Grab" Act
	1875	Secretary of War Belknap resigns to avoid impeachment
	1876	Custer's Last Stand at Little Big Horn
	1877	Rutherford B. Hayes wins Presidency over Samuel Tilden by Special Electoral Commission
SCIENTIFIC	1876	Telephone - Alexander Graham Bell, U.S.
TERRITORY		State admitted: Colorado, 1876

Rutherford B. Hayes

(1822 - 1893) Nineteenth President

BORN	October 4, 1822
PLACE OF BIRTH	Delaware, Ohio
ANCESTRY	English
FATHER	Rutherford Hayes (1787 - 1822)
MOTHER	Sophia Birchard Hayes (1792 - 1866)
WIFE	Lucy Ware Webb (1831 - 1889)
CHILDREN	Eight: 7 boys, 1 girl
EDUCATION	Academy at Norwalk, Ohio; Isaac Webb's School at Middletown, Connecticut; Kenyon College, Gambier, Ohio; Harvard Law School
RELIGION	No formal affiliation
OCCUPATION	Lawyer, soldier
MILITARY SERVICE	Commissioned Major in 23rd Ohio Volunteers (1861), resigned as Major General in June 1865
POLITICAL PARTY	Republican
OFFICES HELD	City Solicitor of Cincinnati; U.S. Congressman; Governor of Ohio
AGE AT INAUGURATION	54
TERMS SERVED	One (1877 - 1881)
VICE PRESIDENT	William A. Wheeler
DIED	January 17, 1893, Fremont, Ohio, age 70
CAUSE OF DEATH	Natural causes

HIGHLIGHTS OF HISTORICAL EVENTS DURING HAYES' ADMINISTRATION (1877 - 1881) (U.S. Population 47,140,727)

POLITICAL	1877	Reconstruction period ends; Federal troops withdrawn from South
	1878	Bland-Allison Act controls silver coinage
	1879	Monetary specie payments resumed
	1880	Garfield elected President
SCIENTIFIC	1876	Microphone - Alexander Graham Bell, U.S.
	1877	Cylindrical phonograph - Thomas A. Edison, U.S.
	1879	First incandescent lamp - Thomas A. Edison, U.S.
	1879	Cash register - James Ritty, U.S.
TERRITORY		No states admitted

James A. Garfield

(1831 - 1881) Twentieth President

BORN	November 19, 1831
PLACE OF BIRTH	Orange (Cuyahoga County) Ohio
ANCESTRY	English, Huguenot
FATHER	Abram Garfield (1799 - 1833)
MOTHER	Eliza Ballou Garfield (1801 - 1888)
WIFE	Lucretia Rudolph (1832 - 1918)
CHILDREN	Seven: 5 boys, 2 girls
EDUCATION	Attended Geauga Academy and Western Reserve Eclectic Institute; graduated from Williams College, Massachusetts
RELIGION	Disciples of Christ
OCCUPATION	Lawyer, soldier, professor, President of Hiram College
MILITARY SERVICE	Commissioned Lieutenant Colonel of 42nd Ohio Volunteers in August 1861; rose to Brigadier General of Volunteers (1862); Major General of Volunteers (1863)
POLITICAL PARTY	Republican
OFFICES HELD	Member of Ohio Senate; Member of U.S. House of Representatives; Chairman of House Committee of Appropriations; Minority Leader in U.S. House of Representatives
AGE AT INAUGURATION	49
TERMS SERVED	One (1881, died in office)
VICE PRESIDENT	Chester A. Arthur
DIED	September 19, 1881, Elberon, New Jersey, age 49
CAUSE OF DEATH	Assassinated

HIGHLIGHTS OF HISTORICAL EVENTS DURING GARFIELD'S ADMINISTRATION (1881 - 1881) (U.S. Population 51,541,575)

POLITICAL	1881	On July 2 President Garfield was shot at the Washington, D.C. railroad station by Charles J. Guiteau. He died on September 19 after serving less than five months in office. On September 20 Vice President Chester A. Arthur took the oath of office as the Nation's 21st President.
SCIENTIFIC	1881	American Red Cross organized under leadership of Clara Barton
TERRITORY		No states admitted

Chester A. Arthur

(1830 - 1886) Twenty-first President

BORN	October 5, 1830
PLACE OF BIRTH	Fairfield, Vermont
ANCESTRY	Scotch-Irish, English
FATHER	William Arthur (1796 - 1875)
MOTHER	Malvina Stone Arthur (1802 - 1869)
WIFE	Ellen Lewis Herndon (1837 - 1880)
CHILDREN	Three: 2 boys, 1 girl
EDUCATION	Attended public schools and Lyceum School; graduated with honors from Union College of Schenectady in 1848
RELIGION	Episcopalian
OCCUPATION	Teacher, school principal, lawyer, Customs official
MILITARY SERVICE	Inspector General of New York troops during Civil War; Quartermaster General for New York State
POLITICAL PARTY	Republican
OFFICES HELD	Engineer-In-Chief, New York State (1861); Collector of Customs, Port of New York (1871); Vice President
AGE AT INAUGURATION	50
TERMS SERVED	One (1881 - 1885)
VICE PRESIDENT	None
DIED	November 18, 1886, New York, New York, age 56
CAUSE OF DEATH	Natural causes

HIGHLIGHTS OF HISTORICAL EVENTS DURING ARTHUR'S ADMINISTRATION (1881 - 1885) (U.S. Population 51,541,575)

POLITICAL	1881	New protective tariff enacted
	1882	Nicaraguan Treaty signed (Panama Canal construction); Chinese Exclusion Act (restricts immigration of Orientals)
	1883	Organization of Civil Service system (Pendleton Act)
	1884	Territorial government established in Alaska
SCIENTIFIC	1881	Wire photo - Shelford Bidwell, England
	1883	Internal combustion engine - Gottlieb Daimler, Germany
	1885	First skyscraper - William Jenney, U.S.
TERRITORY		No states admitted

Grover Cleveland

(1837 - 1908) Twenty-second and Twenty-fourth President

BORN	March 18, 1837
PLACE OF BIRTH	Caldwell, New Jersey
ANCESTRY	English-Scotch, Irish
FATHER	Richard Falley Cleveland (1804 - 1853)
MOTHER	Ann Neal Cleveland (1806 - 1882)
WIFE	Frances Folsom (1864 - 1947)
CHILDREN	Five: 2 boys, 3 girls
EDUCATION	Public schools
RELIGION	Presbyterian
OCCUPATION	Lawyer
MILITARY SERVICE	None
POLITICAL PARTY	Democrat
OFFICES HELD	Erie County Assistant Attorney; Sheriff of Erie County; Mayor of Buffalo; Governor of New York State
AGE AT INAUGURATIONS	47 and 55
TERMS SERVED	Two (1885 - 1889) (1893 - 1897)
VICE PRESIDENTS	Thomas A. Hendricks (1885, died in office) and Adlai E. Stevenson (1893 - 1897)
DIED	June 24, 1908, Princeton, New Jersey, age 71
CAUSE OF DEATH	Natural causes

HIGHLIGHTS OF HISTORICAL EVENTS DURING CLEVELAND'S FIRST ADMINISTRATION (1885 - 1889) (U.S. Population 56,658,347)

POLITICAL	1886	Presidential Succession Act; Treasury surplus grows; American Federation of Labor organized with Samuel Gompers as first President; Statue of Liberty dedicated at Bedloe's Island, New York
	1887	Interstate Commerce Commission formed; Hatch Act
	1888	"Murchison Letter"
	1889	Capture of Apache Chief Geronimo ends South-West Indian hostilities
SCIENTIFIC	1885	Commercial adding machine - William Burroughs, U.S.
	1888	Kodak camera - Eastman Kodak, U.S.
TERRITORY		No states admitted

HIGHLIGHTS OF HISTORICAL EVENTS DURING CLEVELAND'S SECOND ADMINISTRATION (1893 - 1897) (U.S. Population 66,970,496)

POLITICAL	1893	Nationwide bank panic; repeal of Sherman Silver Purchase Act; World Columbian Exposition held in Chicago
	1894	Coxey's Army; Federal troops called out to control Pullman strike
	1896	Hawaii becomes a Republic; McKinley elected President
MILITARY	1895	Cuban revolt
SCIENTIFIC	1894	Wireless telegraph - Guglielmo Marconi, Italy
	1896	Electric Stove - Wm. S. Hadaway, U.S.
TERRITORY		State admitted: Utah, 1896

Benjamin Harrison

(1833 - 1901) Twenty-third President

BORN	August 20, 1833
PLACE OF BIRTH	North Bend, Ohio
ANCESTRY	English-Scotch
FATHER	John Scott Harrison (1804 - 1878)
MOTHER	Elizabeth Irwin Harrison (1810 - 1850)
WIVES	First wife: Caroline ("Carrie") Scott (1832 - 1892)
	Second wife: Mary Scott Lord Dimmick (1858 - 1948)
CHILDREN	First wife, two: 1 boy, 1 girl
	Second wife, one girl
EDUCATION	Private tutoring; attended Farmer's College; graduated Miami University (Ohio), B.A. (1852)
RELIGION	Presbyterian
OCCUPATION	Lawyer, soldier
MILITARY SERVICE	Appointed Colonel in 70th Indiana Volunteers (1862); resigned as Brevet Brigadier General in 1865
POLITICAL PARTY	Republican
OFFICES HELD	Commissioner for the Court of Claims; City Attorney; Secretary of Indiana Republican Central Committee; State Supreme Court Reporter, Member of U.S. Senate
AGE AT INAUGURATION	55
TERMS SERVED	One (1889 - 1893)
VICE PRESIDENT	Levi P. Morton
DIED	March 13, 1901, Indianapolis, Indiana, age 67
CAUSE OF DEATH	Natural causes

HIGHLIGHTS OF HISTORICAL EVENTS DURING HARRISON'S ADMINISTRATION (1889 - 1893) (U.S. Population 61,775,121)

POLITICAL	1889	Pan American Union formed; Oklahoma land rush; Omnibus Bill
	1890	Dependent Pension Act; Sherman Anti-Trust Act passed; Sherman Silver Purchase Act
	1891	Populist Party formed
SCIENTIFIC	1891	Zipper - Whitcomb L. Judson, U.S.
	1892	Electric automobile - William Morrison, U.S.
	1892	Color photography - Frederic E. Ives, U.S.
TERRITORY		States admitted: Montana, North Dakota, South Dakota and Washington, 1889; Idaho and Wyoming, 1890

William McKinley

(1843 - 1901) Twenty-fifth President

BORN	January 29, 1843
PLACE OF BIRTH	Niles, Ohio
ANCESTRY	Scotch-Irish, English
FATHER	William McKinley (1807 - 1892)
MOTHER	Nancy Allison McKinley (1809 - 1897)
WIFE	Ida Saxton (1847 - 1907)
CHILDREN	2 girls
EDUCATION	Attended Poland Academy, Ohio; Allegheny College
RELIGION	Methodist
OCCUPATION	Lawyer, teacher, clerk, soldier
MILITARY SERVICE	Joined Ohio 23rd Volunteers in 1861; rose to rank of Major before leaving Army in 1865
POLITICAL PARTY	Republican
OFFICES HELD	Member of U.S. House of Representatives; Governor of Ohio
AGE AT INAUGURATION	54
TERMS SERVED	Two (1897 - 1901) (1901, died in office)
VICE PRESIDENTS	Garret A. Hobart (1897 - 1899, died in office) and Theodore Roosevelt (1901)
DIED	September 14, 1901, Buffalo, New York, age 58
CAUSE OF DEATH	Assassinated

HIGHLIGHTS OF HISTORICAL EVENTS DURING McKINLEY'S ADMINISTRATION (1897 - 1901) (U.S. Population 72,189,240)

POLITICAL	1897	Gold Rush in Klondike; Dingley Tariff
	1898	Federal Bankruptcy Act; U.S. annexation of Hawaii; Treaty of Paris
	1899	Open Door policy with China; U.S. attends First Hague Conference
	1900	Currency Act; U.S. participation in Boxer Rebellion at Peking
	1901	Platt Amendment; McKinley assassinated in Buffalo, New York, September 6; Theodore Roosevelt takes office
MILITARY	1898	Spanish-American War breaks out (sinking of the Maine in Havana Harbor)
SCIENTIFIC	1900	Underwater submarine - J. P. Holland, U.S.
	1900	Caterpillar tractor - Benjamin Holt, U.S.
TERRITORY	1898	U.S. acquires Puerto Rico, Guam and Philippines from Cuba

Theodore Roosevelt

(1858 - 1919) Twenty-sixth President

BORN	October 27, 1858
PLACE OF BIRTH	New York, New York
ANCESTRY	English, Dutch, Scotch, Huguenot
FATHER	Theodore Roosevelt (1831 - 1878)
MOTHER	Martha Bulloch Roosevelt (1834 - 1884)
WIVES	First wife: Alice Hathaway Lee (1861 - 1884)
	Second wife: Edith Kermit Carow (1861 - 1948)
CHILDREN	First wife, one girl
	Second wife, five: 4 boys, 1 girl
EDUCATION	Private tutoring; 1876 - 1880 Harvard (B.A.); studied law at Columbia
RELIGION	Reformed Dutch
OCCUPATION	Writer, historian, rancher
MILITARY SERVICE	Lieutenant Colonel, Colonel, 1st U.S. Volunteers Cavalry Regiment (Rough Riders) 1898
POLITICAL PARTY	Republican
OFFICES HELD	New York State Assemblyman; U.S. Civil Service Commissioner; President of New York Board of Police Commissioners; Governor of New York State; Assistant Secretary of the Navy; Vice President
AGE AT INAUGURATION	42
TERMS SERVED	Two (1901 - 1905) (1905 - 1909)
VICE PRESIDENT	First term: None. Second term: Charles W. Fairbanks (1905 - 1909)
DIED	January 6, 1919, Oyster Bay, New York, age 60
CAUSE OF DEATH	Heart failure

HIGHLIGHTS OF HISTORICAL EVENTS DURING ROOSEVELT'S ADMINISTRATION (1901 - 1909) (U.S. Population 77,585,000)

POLITICAL	1901	Anti-Trust Act enforced; Newlands Act
	1902	Negotiations opened for acquisition of Panama Canal; Departments of Commerce and Labor created
	1903	Alaskan Boundary Dispute settled
	1904	Corollary to Monroe Doctrine issued
	1905	Roosevelt mediates Russo-Japanese Peace Treaty
	1906	Hepburn Act; Pure Food and Drug Act; earthquake and fire destroy San Francisco
	1907	Financial panic; U.S. Navy sent on voyage around world
	1908	White House Conservation Conference
MILITARY	1904	U.S. intervention in Dominican Republic
SCIENTIFIC	1901	First wireless message sent from Europe
	1903	First successful airplane flight by Wright Brothers at Kitty Hawk
	1905	Theory of relativity - Albert Einstein, Germany
TERRITORY		State admitted: Oklahoma, 1907

William H. Taft

(1857 - 1930) Twenty-seventh President

BORN	September 15, 1857
PLACE OF BIRTH	Cincinnati, Ohio
ANCESTRY	English, Scotch-Irish
FATHER	Alphonso Taft (1810 - 1891)
MOTHER	Louise Torrey Taft (1827 - 1907)
WIFE	Helen (Nellie) Herron (1861 - 1943)
CHILDREN	Three: 2 boys, 1 girl
EDUCATION	Woodward High School, Cincinnati, Ohio; B.A. from Yale University; Cincinnati Law School
RELIGION	Unitarian
OCCUPATION	Lawyer
MILITARY SERVICE	None
POLITICAL PARTY	Republican
OFFICES HELD	Assistant Prosecuting Attorney, Hamilton County, Ohio; Ohio Supreme Court Judge; U.S. Solicitor General; Federal Circuit Court Judge; Civil Governor of Philippines; Secretary of War
AGE AT INAUGURATION	51
TERMS SERVED	One (1909 - 1913)
VICE PRESIDENT	James S. Sherman (1909 - 1912, died in office)
DIED	March 8, 1930, Washington, D.C., age 72
CAUSE OF DEATH	Heart ailment

HIGHLIGHTS OF HISTORICAL EVENTS DURING TAFT'S ADMINISTRATION (1909 - 1913) (U.S. Population 90,492,000)

POLITICAL	1909	Taft opposes Payne-Aldrich Tariff; "Dollar Diplomacy" instituted
	1910	Mann Elkins Act; Postal Savings Act; Boy Scouts of America formed
	1911	Formation of National Progressive Republican League
	1912	Rift costs Taft political support of Teddy Roosevelt; Titanic sunk off Newfoundland
	1913	16th Amendment (Income Tax) ratified
MILITARY	1912	U.S. troops land in Nicaragua to protect American interests during revolt
SCIENTIFIC	1909	Robert E. Peary discovers North Pole
	1909	Helicopter - Igor Sirkorsky, U.S.
	1911	Air conditioning - Willis H. Carrier, U.S.
	1911	Hydroplane - Glenn H. Curtiss, U.S.
TERRITORY		States admitted: New Mexico and Arizona, 1912

Woodrow Wilson

(1856 - 1924) Twenty-eighth President

BORN	December 28, 1856
PLACE OF BIRTH	Staunton, Virginia
ANCESTRY	Scotch-Irish
FATHER	Joseph Ruggles Wilson (1822 - 1903)
MOTHER	Janet (Jessie) Woodrow Wilson (1836 - 1888)
WIVES	First wife: Ellen Louise Axson (1860 - 1914)
	Second wife: Edith Bolling Galt (1872 - 1961)
CHILDREN	Three girls (first marriage)
EDUCATION	Private tutors; Davidson College; Princeton University; University of Virginia Law School; Ph.D. (1886) Johns Hopkins University
RELIGION	Presbyterian
OCCUPATION	Lawyer, historian, professor, President of Princeton University
MILITARY SERVICE	None
POLITICAL PARTY	Democrat
OFFICE HELD	Governor of New Jersey
AGE AT INAUGURATION	56
TERMS SERVED	Two (1913 - 1917) (1917 - 1921)
VICE PRESIDENT	Thomas Marshall (both terms)
DIED	February 3, 1924, Washington, D.C., age 67
CAUSE OF DEATH	Natural causes

HIGHLIGHTS OF HISTORICAL EVENTS DURING WILSON'S ADMINISTRATION (1913 - 1921) (U.S. Population 97,227,000)

POLITICAL	1913	17th Amendment ratified; Federal Reserve Act
	1914	Death of Mrs. Wilson; U.S. declares neutrality; Federal Trade Commission Act; Clayton Anti-Trust Act
	1915	Sinking of Lusitania
	1916	National Defense Act; Federal Farm Loan Act; Adamson Act; Keating-Owen Act (Child Labor Law)
	1917	War Industries Board established; diplomatic relations with Germany ended; Liberty Loan Act; Selective Serivce Act; Espionage Act
	1918	Wilson issues his Fourteen Points for Peace
	1919	Wilson awarded Nobel Peace Prize; Congress enacts Prohibition (18th Amendment)
	1920	Senate rejects entry into League of Nations; 19th Amendment (women's right to vote) ratified; first meeting of League of Nations; Senate refuses to ratify Treaty of Versailles
MILITARY	1914	Pancho Villas' forces dominate Mexican Revolution
	1915	Wilson orders troops into Veracruz, led by General John J. Pershing
	1917	Congress declares war on Germany April 6; Germany torpedoes U.S. shipping on high seas; General Pershing heads American expeditionary forces
	1918	November 11, World War I Armistice; Germany surrenders
SCIENTIFIC	1915	Transcontinental telephone service begins on regular basis
	1916	Thompson submachine gun - John T. Thompson, U.S.
	1917	Submarine detector - Max Mason, U.S.
	1921	First transcontinental airmail flight
TERRITORY	1917	U.S. purchases Virgin Islands from Denmark

Warren G. Harding

(1865 - 1923) Twenty-ninth President

BORN	November 2, 1865
PLACE OF BIRTH	Blooming Grove, Ohio
ANCESTRY	English, Scotch-Irish
FATHER	George Tryon Harding (? - 1928)
MOTHER	Phoebe Dickerson Harding (1843 - 1910)
WIFE	Florence Kling DeWolfe (1860 - 1924)
CHILDREN	None
EDUCATION	Local schools; Ohio Central College
RELIGION	Baptist
OCCUPATION	Newspaper editor and publisher
POLITICAL PARTY	Republican
OFFICES HELD	Member of Ohio Senate; Lt. Governor of Ohio; U.S. Senator
AGE AT INAUGURATION	55
TERMS SERVED	One (1921 - 1923, died in office)
VICE PRESIDENT	Calvin Coolidge
DIED	August 2, 1923, San Francisco, California, age 57
CAUSE OF DEATH	Stroke

HIGHLIGHTS OF HISTORICAL EVENTS DURING HARDING'S ADMINISTRATION (1921 - 1923) (U.S. Population 105,541,000)

POLITICAL	1921	U.S. Budget Bureau formed; Washington Armament Conference (Naval Disarmament)
	1922	Capper-Volstead Act; Second Central American Conference
	1923	Intermediate Credit Act; Teapot Dome Scandals rock Harding's Administration; Harding dies in office August 2 while visiting San Francisco; Coolidge takes oath August 3
MILITARY	1922	U.S. Veterans Bureau established
SCIENTIFIC	1922	Technicolor process - Herbert T. Kalmus, U.S.
	1922	Radar - Albert H. Taylor and Leo C. Young, U.S.
	1923	Motion picture sound film - Thomas A. Edison, U.S.
TERRITORY	No states admitted	

Calvin Coolidge

(1872 - 1933) Thirtieth President

BORN	July 4, 1872
PLACE OF BIRTH	Plymouth Notch, Vermont
ANCESTRY	English
FATHER	John Calvin Coolidge (1845 - 1926)
MOTHER	Victoria Josphine Moor Coolidge (1846 - 1885)
WIFE	Grace Anna Goodhue (1879 - 1957)
CHILDREN	Two boys
EDUCATION	Plymouth District School; Black River Academy; St. Johnsbury Academy; Amherst College
RELIGION	Congregationalist
OCCUPATION	Lawyer
MILITARY SERVICE	None
POLITICAL PARTY	Republican
OFFICES HELD	Member of Massachusetts House of Representatives; Mayor of Northampton, Massachusetts; Member and President of Massachusetts Senate; Lt. Governor of Massachusetts; Governor of Massachusetts; Vice President
AGE AT INAUGURATION	51
TERMS SERVED	Two (1923 - 1925, completed Harding's term) (1925 - 1929)
VICE PRESIDENT	Charles G. Dawes (1925 - 1929)
DIED	January 5, 1933, Northampton, Massachusetts, age 60
CAUSE OF DEATH	Coronary thrombosis

HIGHLIGHTS OF HISTORICAL EVENTS DURING COOLIDGE'S ADMINISTRATION (1923 - 1929) (U.S. Population 111,950,000)

POLITICAL	1923	Dawes Plan
	1924	World War I Veterans Benefits (Soldier's Bonus Act); J. Edgar Hoover appointed head of F.B.I.
	1925	Scopes Trial
	1926	Revenue Act; citizenship granted to U.S.-born Indians
	1927	Geneva Convention; Charles A. Lindbergh makes first solo non-stop flight from New York to Paris; defeat of McNary-Haugen Bill
	1928	Merchant Marine Act; Kellogg-Briand Pact outlaws war
MILITARY	1925	Billy Mitchell court martial
SCIENTIFIC	1923	Television iconoscope scanner - Vladimir K. Zworykin, U.S.
	1926	First flight over North Pole - Richard E. Byrd, U.S.
TERRITORY	No states admitted	

Herbert Hoover

(1874 - 1964) Thirty-first President

BORN	August 10, 1874
PLACE OF BIRTH	West Branch, Iowa
ANCESTRY	German-Swiss, English
FATHER	Jesse Clark Hoover (1846 - 1880)
MOTHER	Huldah Randall Minthorn Hoover (1849 - 1883)
WIFE	Lou Henry (1875 - 1944)
CHILDREN	Two boys
EDUCATION	Local schools; Newberg Academy; graduated from Stanford University (1895)
RELIGION	Quaker
OCCUPATION	Engineer
MILITARY SERVICE	None
POLITICAL PARTY	Republican
OFFICES HELD	Chairman of Commission for Relief in Belgium; U.S. Food Administrator; Chairman of Supreme Economic Council; Secretary of Commerce
AGE AT INAUGURATION	54
TERMS SERVED	One (1929-1933)
VICE PRESIDENT	Charles Curtis (1929 - 1933)
DIED	October 20, 1964, New York, New York, age 90
CAUSE OF DEATH	Natural causes

HIGHLIGHTS OF HISTORICAL EVENTS DURING HOOVER'S ADMINISTRATION (1929 - 1933) (U.S. Population 121,770,000)

POLITICAL	1928	Agricultural Marketing Act
	1929	Stock Market Crash creates panic and nationwide depression; run on banks
	1930	Hoover Relief Policy; Veteran's Administration established; Hawley-Smoot Tariff
	1931	Wickersham Report on 18th Amendment
	1932	Reconstruction Finance Corporation established; "Bonus Army" marches on Washington
	1933	20th Amendment ratified ("Lame Duck")
SCIENTIFIC	1928	Computer (differential analyzer) - Vannevar Bush, U.S.
	1932	Polarized glass lens - Edwin H. Land, U.S.
TERRITORY	No states admitted	

Franklin D. Roosevelt

(1882 - 1945) Thirty-second President

BORN	January 30, 1882
PLACE OF BIRTH	Hyde Park, New York
ANCESTRY	Dutch, Huguenot, English
FATHER	James Roosevelt (1828 - 1900)
MOTHER	Sara Delano Roosevelt (1854 - 1941)
WIFE	Anna Eleanor (1884 - 1962)
CHILDREN	Five: 4 boys, 1 girl
EDUCATION	Private tutor; Groton School; B.A. Harvard University; studied law at Columbia University
RELIGION	Episcopalian
OCCUPATION	Lawyer
MILITARY SERVICE	None
POLITICAL PARTY	Democrat
OFFICES HELD	Member of New York State Senate; Assistant Secretary of the Navy; Governor of New York
AGE AT INAUGURATION	51
TERMS SERVED	Four (1933 - 1937) (1937 - 1941) (1941 - 1945) (1945, died in office)
VICE PRESIDENTS	John Garner (1933 - 1937) (1937 - 1941) Henry Wallace (1941 - 1945) and Harry S. Truman (1945)
DIED	April 12, 1945, Warm Springs, Georgia, age 63
CAUSE OF DEATH	Cerebral hemorrhage

HIGHLIGHTS OF HISTORICAL EVENTS DURING ROOSEVELT'S ADMINISTRATION (1933 - 1945) (U.S. Population 125,579,000)

POLITICAL	1933	New Deal Recovery Reforms; Emergency Banking Relief Act; Agricultural Adjustment Act; Federal Securities Act; Federal Bank Deposit Insurance Corp.; Public Works Administration
	1934	Export-Import Bank; Gold Reserve Act; Securities and Exchange Commission
	1935	Civilian Conservation Corps; National Labor Relations Board; Second New Deal Policy; Works Progress Administration; Social Security Act; Unemployment and Old Age Compensation Acts
	1936	Soil Conservation Act; Robinson Patman Act; Merchant Marine Act; Roosevelt wins nomination and election
	1937	Miller-Tydings Act; National Housing Act; Roosevelt calls special session of Congress
	1938	Ludlow Resolution to increase U.S. armaments; Food, Drug and Cosmetic Act (Wheeler-Lea Act)
	1940	Alien Registration Act (Smith Act); Selective Training and Service Act; Office of Defense Production
	1941	FDR's "Four Freedoms"; Lend Lease Act for Allies; State of National Emergency proclaimed; FDR confers with Churchill and announces Atlantic Charter; FDR first President to run for third term
	1942	U.S. and 26 countries sign United Nations declaration; War Production Board established
	1944	Roosevelt runs for fourth term and defeats Thomas E. Dewey; Harry S. Truman elected Vice President
	1945	FDR meets with Stalin and Churchill at Yalta
MILITARY	1939	World War II begins
	1941	Germany invades Russia; December 7 Japan attacks Pearl Harbor; U.S. declares war on Japan; Germany and Italy declare war on U.S.
	1943	U.S. naval forces in South Pacific begin offensive; invasion of Sicily; invasion of Italy
	1944	Allies land in France ("Invasion of Normandy"); U.S. forces march on Germany; Battle of the Bulge
	1945	U.S. troops recapture Philippines from Japanese; Allies cross Rhine
SCIENTIFIC	1937	Nylon - Wallace H. Carothers, U.S.; Jet engine - Frank Whittle, England; Electronic computer - Howard Aiken, U.S.
	1942	First successful nuclear reaction achieved at University of Chicago
TERRITORY	1940	U.S. acquires 99-year leases on air and naval bases in the British West Indies from England

Harry S. Truman

(1884 - 1972) Thirty-third President

BORN	May 8, 1884
PLACE OF BIRTH	Lamar, Missouri
ANCESTRY	English, Scotch-Irish
FATHER	John Anderson Truman (1851 - 1914)
MOTHER	Martha Ellen Young Truman (1852 - 1947)
WIFE	Elizabeth Virginia Wallace (1885 -1982)
CHILDREN	One girl
EDUCATION	Graduated from Public High School
RELIGION	Baptist
OCCUPATION	Railroad time keeper, bank clerk, haberdasher, farmer
MILITARY SERVICE	Missouri National Guard; Captain in 129th Field Artillery (1918 - 1919)
POLITICAL PARTY	Democrat
OFFICES HELD	County Judge for Eastern District of Jackson County Missouri; Presiding Judge, County Court, Jackson County Missouri; U.S. Senator; Vice President
AGE AT INAUGURATION	60
TERMS SERVED	Two (1945 - 1949, completed Roosevelt's term) (1949 - 1953)
VICE PRESIDENT	Alben Barkley (1949 - 1953)
DIED	December 26, 1972, Kansas City, Missouri, age 88
CAUSE OF DEATH	Natural causes

HIGHLIGHTS OF HISTORICAL EVENTS DURING TRUMAN'S ADMINISTRATION (1945 - 1953) (U.S. Population 132,481,000)

POLITICAL	1945	First United Nations International Conference held in San Francisco; Potsdam Conference; Truman's Fair Deal Program
	1946	Atomic Energy Commission established; Paris Peace Conference; Truman defeats Dewey for second term
	1947	Truman Doctrine; Taft Hartley Act passed; Marshall Plan (aid to European countries) established; beginning of "Cold War"
	1948	Whittaker Chambers and Alger Hiss trial; Berlin blockade and airlift
	1949	Truman's Point Four Program; North Atlantic Treaty Organization (NATO)
	1950	Internal Security Act (McCarran Act); assassination attempt on Truman
	1951	Japanese Peace Treaty signed; 22nd Amendment passed; Kefauver Hearings
	1952	McCarthy Hearings; Bricker Amendment
MILITARY	1945	May 8 V.E. Day; Germany unconditionally surrenders; U.S. drops atomic bomb on Hiroshima and Nagasaki; Japan surrenders August 14
	1950	Korean War starts; U.S. troops sent to South Korea to repel Communist invaders
SCIENTIFIC	1945	Atomic bomb first detonated by international team of scientists
	1948	Long playing (LP) record - Peter C. Goldmark, U.S.
	1948	Zerography - Chester Carlson, U.S.
	1951	First transcontinental TV broadcast

Dwight D. Eisenhower

(1890 - 1969) Thirty-fourth President

BORN	October 14, 1890
PLACE OF BIRTH	Denison, Texas
ANCESTRY	Swiss-German
FATHER	David Jacob Eisenhower (1863 - 1942)
MOTHER	Ida Elizabeth Stover Eisenhower (1862 - 1946)
WIFE	Mamie Geneva Doud (1896–1979)
CHILDREN	Two boys
EDUCATION	Public Schools; U.S. Military Academy (West Point, New York), graduated 1915
RELIGION	Presbyterian
OCCUPATION	Soldier; President of Columbia University (1948 - 1951)
MILITARY SERVICE	Commissioned Second Lieutenant in U.S. Army (1915); served in various posts in U.S., Panama, and Philippines (1915 - 1942); named Commander of European Theater of Operations (1942); named Supreme Commander of Allied Expeditionary Force in Western Europe (1943); promoted to General of the Army (1944); named Army Chief of Staff (1945); appointed Supreme Commander of Allied powers in Europe (1951)
POLITICAL PARTY	Republican
OFFICES HELD	None
AGE AT INAUGURATION	62
TERMS SERVED	Two (1953 - 1957) (1957 - 1961)
VICE PRESIDENT	Richard M. Nixon (both terms)
DIED	March 28, 1969, Walter Reed Hospital, Washington, D.C., age 78
CAUSE OF DEATH	Heart failure

HIGHLIGHTS OF HISTORICAL EVENTS DURING EISENHOWER'S ADMINISTRATION (1953 - 1961) (U.S. Population 158,434,000)

POLITICAL	1953	Eisenhower becomes first Republican President since 1928; Eisenhower travels to Korea; Earl Warren named Chief Justice
	1954	Supreme Court orders racial desegregation of schools; Army-McCarthy Hearings; U.S. supplies French with air support in Indochina; Southeast Asia Treaty Organization (SEATO) signed
	1955	Department of Health, Education and Welfare formed; Eisenhower attends Summit Conference in Geneva (Geneva Accords); Eisenhower suffers heart attack; AFL-CIO merge into single labor union
	1956	Bus boycott in Montgomery, Alabama, brings Dr. Martin Luther King into national prominence; Suez crisis; Eisenhower defeats Adlai E. Stevenson for Presidency second time
	1957	Civil Rights Commission established; Eisenhower Doctrine; Federal troops ordered into Little Rock, Arkansas; Eisenhower suffers stroke
	1958	U.S. troops sent to Lebanon; NASA created
	1959	Eisenhower and Khrushchev meet at Camp David, Md.; Fidel Castro rises to power in Cuba
	1960	U-2 incident; St. Lawrence Seaway opened
MILITARY	1953	Korean Armistice
SCIENTIFIC	1953	Polio vaccine - Dr. Jonas Salk, U.S.
	1957	Sputnik I launched by Soviet Union
	1958	First U.S. earth satellite launched
	1960	Laser - Charles A. Townes, U.S.
TERRITORY		States admitted: Hawaii and Alaska, 1959

John F. Kennedy

(1917 - 1963) Thirty-fifth President

BORN	May 29, 1917
PLACE OF BIRTH	Brookline, Massachusetts
ANCESTRY	Irish
FATHER	Joseph Patrick Kennedy (1888 - 1969)
MOTHER	Rose Fitzgerald Kennedy (1891 -)
WIFE	Jacqueline Lee Bouvier (1929 -)
CHILDREN	Three: 2 boys, 1 girl
EDUCATION	Attended the Choate School; London School of Economics; Princeton University; graduated Harvard (1940); Stanford University
RELIGION	Roman Catholic
OCCUPATION	Author, reporter
MILITARY SERVICE	Ensign, Lieutenant (J.G.), U.S. Naval Reserve (active duty 1941 - 1945)
POLITICAL PARTY	Democrat
OFFICES HELD	Member of U.S. House of Representatives; Member of U.S. Senate
AGE AT INAUGURATION	43
TERMS SERVED	One (1961 - 1963, died in office)
VICE PRESIDENT	Lyndon B. Johnson
DIED	November 22, 1963, Dallas, Texas, age 46
CAUSE OF DEATH	Assassinated

HIGHLIGHTS OF HISTORICAL EVENTS DURING KENNEDY'S ADMINISTRATION (1961 - 1963) (U.S. Population 183,650,000)

POLITICAL	1961	Formation of Peace Corps; Alliance for Progress in Latin America; invasion of Cuba by U.S.-supported exiles fails (Bay of Pigs); Kennedy meets with DeGaulle, Khrushchev and MacMillan in Europe; Kennedy declares continued U.S. support for Vietnam Independence
	1962	Kennedy asks Russia to join U.S. in mutual space exploration; steel companies forced to retract price increase; Federal troops sent to University of Mississippi to enforce Negro admissions; Trade Expansion Act; Kennedy confronts Russian missile threat in Cuba; Kennedy orders end to racial discrimination in Federal housing
	1963	Federal troops ordered to put down race riots in Birmingham, Ala.; Kennedy signs Nuclear Test Ban Treaty with Great Britain and Russia; Kennedy achieves peaceful integration of students in University of Alabama; march on Washington, D.C. by Civil Rights groups; Kennedy assassinated in Dallas, Texas, November 22
MILITARY	1961	U.S. sends military aid to Laos
	1963	U.S. military support strengthened in Vietnam
SCIENTIFIC	1961	Russia's Yuri Gagarin first man to orbit earth; U.S. Astronauts Shepard and Grissom make sub-orbital space flights
	1962	Lieutenant Colonel John Glenn makes first U.S. orbit of earth
	1963	Major Cooper of U.S. orbits earth 22 times

Lyndon B. Johnson

(1908 - 1973) Thirty-sixth President

BORN	August 27, 1908
PLACE OF BIRTH	Near Stonewall, Texas
ANCESTRY	English
FATHER	Samuel Ealy Johnson (1877 - 1937)
MOTHER	Rebekah Baines Johnson (1881 - 1958)
WIFE	Claudia Alta Taylor ("Lady Bird") (1912 -)
CHILDREN	Two girls
EDUCATION	Johnson City High School; B.S. (1930) Southwest Texas State Teacher's College; attended Georgetown University Law School
RELIGION	Disciples of Christ
OCCUPATION	School teacher, rancher
MILITARY SERVICE	Lieutenant Commander; Commander, U.S. Naval Reserve (active duty 1941 - 1942)
POLITICAL PARTY	Democrat
OFFICES HELD	National Youth Administration Director in Texas; Member of U.S. House of Representatives; Member of U.S. Senate; Vice President
AGE AT INAUGURATION	55
TERMS SERVED	Two (1963 - 1965, completed Kennedy's term) (1965 - 1969)
VICE PRESIDENT	Hubert Humphrey
DIED	January 22, 1973, San Antonio, Texas, age 64
CAUSE OF DEATH	Natural causes

HIGHLIGHTS OF HISTORICAL EVENTS DURING JOHNSON'S ADMINISTRATION (1963 - 1969) (U.S. Population 189,417,000)

POLITICAL	1963	LBJ appoints Warren Commission to investigate Kennedy assassination
	1964	24th Amendment abolishing poll tax is ratified; LBJ announces his "War on Poverty"; Office of Economic Opportunity created; Johnson defeats Senator Barry Goldwater by wide margin in Presidential election; Civil Rights legislation passed on school segregation
	1965	Serious race riots break out in Watts section of Los Angeles; LBJ steps up military aid to South Vietnam; revolution in Dominican Republic; LBJ signs Medicare and Voting Rights Acts
	1966	LBJ meets with Premier Ky in Honolulu; LBJ attends Manila Conference on Vietnam; race riots break out in Chicago, Cleveland and other cities
	1967	LBJ meets with Premier Kosygin in Glassboro, N.J.; Thurgood Marshall named to Supreme Court; anti-war, anti-draft protests increase
	1968	LBJ announces decision not to seek re-election; Dr. Martin Luther King assassinated in Memphis; Senator Robert F. Kennedy assassinated in Los Angeles; preliminary Paris Peace Talks begin; Richard M. Nixon defeats Hubert Humphrey in Presidential election
MILITARY	1964	North Vietnamese torpedo boats attack U.S. destroyers; LBJ orders bombing of North Vietnam
	1965	U.S. troops sent to Dominican Republic to quell revolution
	1966	U.S. bombs Hanoi
	1968	North Korea seizes U.S. Navy intelligence ship Pueblo, crew imprisoned for eleven months
SCIENTIFIC	1965	Commercial communications satellite - U.S. scientific team
	1966	First "U.S. soft landing" on Moon
	1967	First human heart transplant - Dr. Christian Barnard, South Africa
	1967	Evidence dating man's origin 2-1/2 million years - discovered by team of Harvard archaeologists in Kenya

Richard M. Nixon

(1913 -) Thirty-seventh President

BORN	January 9, 1913
PLACE OF BIRTH	Yorba Linda, California
ANCESTRY	English-Scotch, Irish
FATHER	Francis Anthony Nixon (1878 - 1956)
MOTHER	Hannah Milhous (1885 - 1967)
WIFE	Thelma Patricia Ryan (1913 -)
CHILDREN	Two girls
EDUCATION	Whittier High School; B.A. (1934) Whittier College; L.L.B. (1937) Duke University Law School
RELIGION	Quaker
OCCUPATION	Lawyer
MILITARY SERVICE	Lieutenant (J.G.), Lieutenant Commander, U.S. Navy; Commander U.S. Naval Reserve (active duty, 1942 - 1946)
POLITICAL PARTY	Republican
OFFICES HELD	Member of U.S. House of Representatives; Member of U.S. Senate; Vice President
AGE AT INAUGURATION	56
TERMS SERVED	(1969 - 1974 r*)
VICE PRESIDENT	Spiro Agnew r*, Gerald R. Ford
	r - resigned

HIGHLIGHTS OF HISTORICAL EVENTS DURING NIXON'S ADMINISTRATION (1969-1974)
(U.S. Population 202,253,000)

POLITICAL	1969	Nixon formulates policy of gradual troop withdrawl from Vietnam; Congress approves draft reform
	1970	Vietnamization plan effected to wind-down the war
	1971	National Guard sent to Kent State University to control student riots; Daniel Ellsberg discloses Pentagon Papers; Wage-Price controls enacted
	1972	Historic visit to Peking for meeting with Premier Chow En-lai and Mao Tse-tung; constitutionality of school busing contested in state courts; Moscow Summit Conference; five men arrested and charged with burglarizing Democratic National Committee headquarters in Watergate Hotel
	1973	Special prosecutor appointed to investigate Watergate Affair; Spiro Agnew resigns in October after an investigation into pay-offs and charges of tax evasion; energy crisis develops in U.S. as a result of Arab oil policies
	1974	Judiciary Committee recommends three Articles of Impeachment; August 9, President Nixon resigns
MILITARY	1970	U.S. ground forces move into Cambodia and Laos
	1972	U.S. increases air strikes over North Vietnam
	1973	Negotiated cease-fire signed in Vietnam; prisoners of war return home; Mid-east erupts into ''The Yom Kippur War'' after Egypt and Syria attack Israel
SCIENTIFIC	1969	U.S. Astronauts Neil Armstrong and Edwin Aldrin make first moon walk
	1973	U.S. launches Skylab, first manned space station

Gerald R. Ford

(1913 -) Thirty-eighth President

BORN	July 14, 1913 (named Leslie King at birth)
PLACE OF BIRTH	Omaha, Nebraska
ANCESTRY	Scotch-English
FATHER	Leslie King (-)
	Gerald R. Ford, Sr. (1890-1962) (Mother's second husband, who legally adopted her son in 1918, when his name was changed from Leslie King to Gerald R. Ford)
MOTHER	Dorothy Gardner (1892-1967)
WIFE	Elizabeth Bloomer (1918 -)
CHILDREN	Four: three boys, one girl
EDUCATION	South High School, Grand Rapids, Michigan; B.A. (1935) University of Michigan; L.L.B. (1941) Yale University Law School
RELIGION	Episcopalian
OCCUPATION	Lawyer
MILITARY SERVICE	Lieutenant Commander, U.S. Navy (active duty, 1942-1946)
POLITICAL PARTY	Republican
OFFICES HELD	Member U.S. House of Representatives; Minority Leader, House of Representatives; Vice President
AGE AT INAUGURATION	61
TERMS SERVED	(1974 - 1977, to complete Nixon's term)
VICE PRESIDENT	Nelson A. Rockefeller

HIGHLIGHTS OF HISTORICAL EVENTS DURING FORD'S ADMINISTRATION (1974-1977)
(U.S. Population, est. 213,110,000)

POLITICAL	1974	Ford pardons Richard Nixon for any federal crimes he may have committed as president; Ford calls a Summit conference with top U.S. economists to formulate anti-inflation programs
	1975	Secretary of State Henry Kissinger travels to seven countries in "shuttle diplomacy" trying to achieve world peace
MILITARY	1975	Arabs accuse Israel of premeditated air attacks, U.S. protests before United Nations
SCIENTIFIC	1975	U.S. Apollo and USSR Soyuz linked for visit in space
	1976	Viking I makes first successful landing on Mars

Sam Patrick

James E. Carter, Jr.

(1924 -) Thirty-ninth President

BORN   October 1, 1924
PLACE OF BIRTH   Plains, Georgia
ANCESTRY   Irish
FATHER   James Earl Carter, Sr. (1894-1953)
MOTHER   Lillian Gordy (1898 - 1983)
WIFE   Rosalynn Smith (1927 -)
CHILDREN   Four: three boys, one girl
EDUCATION   Plains High School, Plains, Georgia Southwestern
                         College; Georgia Institute of Technology; B.S. (1947)
                         United States Naval Academy; Union College
RELIGION   Baptist
OCCUPATION   Farmer, warehouseman, businessman
MILITARY SERVICE   Lieutenant Commander, U.S. Navy (1946-1953)
POLITICAL PARTY   Democrat
OFFICES HELD   Member Georgia State Senate; Governor of Georgia
AGE AT INAUGURATION   52
TERMS SERVED   One (1977-1981)
VICE PRESIDENT   Walter Mondale

HIGHLIGHTS OF HISTORICAL EVENTS DURING CARTER'S ADMINISTRATION (1977-1981)
(U.S. Population, est. 221,000,000)

POLITICAL   1977   Carter grants full pardon to most Vietnam draft evaders
             1978   Senate ratifies Panama Canal Treaty which returns control of Canal to Panama by 1999; five Americans killed in Jonestown, Guyana just before 900 religious cult members die in mass suicide
             1979   U.S. establishes diplomatic relations with Communist China; accident at Three Mile Island Nuclear Plant results in radiation leak and evacuation of immediate area; inflation continues to rise; severe shortage of oil due to increase in OPEC prices

MILITARY   1978   Carter joins Israel and Egypt in Camp David Talks which result in signing of Peace Treaty
             1979   U.S. and Soviet Union complete draft treaty to limit nuclear weapons (SALT II)

SCIENTIFIC   1979   Unmanned Skylab space station falls, showering earth with pieces of the spacecraft - no injuries reported

Ronald W. Reagan

(1911 -   ) Fortieth President

BORN	February 6, 1911
PLACE OF BIRTH	Tampico, Illinois
ANCESTRY	Irish-Scotch-English
FATHER	John Edward Reagan (1883 - 1941)
MOTHER	Nelly Clyde Wilson (1883 - 1962)
WIFE	Nancy Davis (1924 -)
CHILDREN	Four: one girl and an adopted boy from his first marriage to actress Jane Wyman, one girl and one boy from his second marriage to Nancy Davis.
EDUCATION	Dixon High School; B.A. (1932) Eureka College (Illinois)
RELIGION	Christian Church
OCCUPATION	Businessman, rancher, actor
MILITARY SERVICE	Second Lieutenant, U.S. Army Reserve; Captain, USAF (active duty, 1942 - 1945)
POLITICAL PARTY	Republican
OFFICES HELD	Governor of California; President, Screen Actors Guild; Chairman Motion Picture Industry Council
AGE AT INAUGURATION	69
TERMS SERVED	Two (1981 - 1985) (1985 -)
VICE PRESIDENT	George Bush

HIGHLIGHTS OF HISTORICAL EVENTS DURING REAGAN'S ADMINISTRATION (1981–   ) (U.S. Population, est. 222,895,548)

POLITICAL	Mar. 30, 1981	After a speech to the AFL-CIO at the Hilton Hotel in Washington, D.C., President Reagan is hit by a would-be assassin's bullet. The President undergoes successful surgery for the removal of the bullet.
	Jul. 7, 1981	President Reagan nominates Judge Sandra Day O'Connor as the first woman Supreme Court justice.
	Mar. 14, 1982	The Reagan Administration authorizes Mexico to make proposals to normalize U.S. relations with Cuba and Nicaragua and for ending what it continues to charge is outside support for leftist insurgents in the Salvadoran civil war.
	Jan. 5, 1983	President Reagan nominates Elizabeth Dole as Secretary of Transportation. Dole, 46, has been working in the White House as presidential assistant for public liaison.
	Jul. 19, 1984	The Democratic Party holds its convention in San Francisco and nominates Walter Mondale for president and Geraldine Ferraro as vice-president. Ferraro is the first woman to be so nominated.
	Aug. 22, 1984	President Reagan and Vice-President Bush are renominated to carry the Republican party standard in Dallas, Texas at the Republican convention.
	Nov. 6, 1984	President Reagan is re-elected to office for another four years in a landslide victory.
MILITARY	Aug. 20, 1982	President Reagan orders about 800 marines to Lebanon to participate with French and Italian forces to supervise the withdrawal of Palestinian and Syrian fighters from Beirut.
	Sep. 1, 1983	An unarmed South Korean jumbo jet carrying 269 people is shot down by a Soviet fighter plane near the Soviet island of Sakhalin.
	Oct. 23, 1983	Over 200 American military—members of the multinational peace keeping force in Lebanon—are killed in a terrorist attack at the marine compound at the Beirut airport in Lebanon.
	Oct. 25, 1983	President Reagan announces the U.S. invasion of Grenada "to assist in a joint effort to restore order and democracy."
	Nov. 2, 1983	Hostilities are successfully ended in Grenada and American forces begin to withdraw.
	Feb. 7, 1984	President Reagan announces plans to begin withdrawal of American troops from Lebanon.
SCIENTIFIC	Apr. 12, 1981	Six Columbia space shuttles are launched between this date and November 28, 1983.
	Apr. 4, 1983	Five Challenger space shuttles are launched between this date and April 6, 1984.
	Aug. 30, 1984	Three Discovery space shuttles are launched between this date and January 24, 1985.

The White House

A History of the White House

Every president, with the exception of George Washington, has lived at 1600 Pennsylvania Avenue. Plans for the construction of what was then known as the President's House began during George Washington's administration — as did plans for the entire city of Washington, D.C. The President's House was to be both a suitable dwelling for the chief executive and a place where foreign rulers and diplomats could be received in style.

The Commissioners of the Federal City (Washington) established two architectural competitions in 1791. By July, 1792, a gold medal was awarded to James Hoban, a resident of Charleston, South Carolina, for his designs of the mansion. The exterior design reflected the Palladian architecture of mid-18th century Europe, but the house was to undergo many changes from Hoban's original plans.

Although the work progressed slowly, President John Adams was able to move to Washington in June, 1800. He moved into the unfinished mansion on November 1 of that same year.

Mrs. Abigail Adams described the uncompleted President's House in a letter to her daughter:

"The house is made habitable but there is not a single apartment finished. . . . We have not the least fence, yard or other convenience, without, and the great unfinished audience-room" (today the East Room) "I make a drying room of, to hang up the clothes in. The principal stairs are not up and will not be this winter."

Thomas Jefferson described the house as, "Big enough for two emperors, one Pope and the grand lama." Architect Benjamin Henry Latrobe was hired by Jefferson to assist him in completing the unfinished building. Latrobe was responsible for changes in Hoban's original design. The influence of Jefferson's preferences appeared as pavilions and elegant terraces which concealed such functional necessities as hen houses, laundry rooms and storerooms.

Inside the mansion, Jefferson decorated with ideas from the continent. Where Adams' taste was decidedly English, Jefferson preferred French furnishings as well as French food. This trend toward elegance was continued by Dolley Madison, the wife of President James Madison.

Many of the early furnishings at the President's House were lost in the burning of Washington during the War of 1812. The big house would have been totally destroyed by that fire in 1814 if it weren't for a providential rainstorm which put out the flames. In rebuilding the burned-out shell, white paint was used on the exterior to cover the traces of the fire. The name "White House" was not officially adopted until 1901, but it was known as the White House from 1816 on.

By 1816, President James Monroe moved into the mansion — now rebuilt but still largely unfurnished. New furniture was ordered and, as the decade of the 1820s proceeded, the White House was again an elegant place for the President to live and receive the nation's guests.

As the 19th century progressed, the country's presidents — as well as their wives — left their mark on the building at 1600 Pennsylvania Avenue. Mrs. Abraham Lincoln was publicly criticized for the amount of Federal money used to improve the White House during the Civil War. Mrs. Grover Cleveland was married in the White House, and Mrs. Benjamin Harrison collected examples of the china used by previous administrations.

When Theodore Roosevelt became president, his wife and six children took up residence in the White House. It was a time of pony rides, wrestling matches and children's voices echoing in the high-ceilinged rooms. But it was also a time of change. Mrs. Roosevelt hired architects to handle a major remodeling of the building in 1902. This remodeling was a return to the simple, classical lines of the original building.

During World War I, grazing flocks of sheep were seen on the White House lawn — an attempt by President Woodrow Wilson to release needed men for the war effort.

By 1927, the roof of the White House was in need of repair. Under President Calvin Coolidge, the roof was raised high enough to add an extra floor onto the mansion. This renovation actually weakened the structure, and President Truman ordered extensive remodeling and repairs which began in 1949 and were completed in 1952. These were the last major repairs done on the White House to date.

Inside the White House

In this brief history of the White House, it is not possible to describe the entire mansion. All of the presidents who have lived here have left something of themselves in this, the most famous house in the United States. The visitor to Washington, D.C. who takes a tour of the White House will surely see some of the rooms listed below. If he sees all of them, he is most fortunate to have walked the same halls as all but one of the Presidents of the United States.

The East Room

One of the first rooms the visitor to the White House will see is the elegant East Room, decorated in white and gold with shining parquet floors. In this room, official receptions are held as well as some news conferences. Here, too, the seven presidents who died in office laid in state.

When the President holds formal dinners in the State Dining Room and plans entertainment afterward, this entertainment is frequently held in the East Room — a suitable setting for plays, concerts and recitals. The modern East Room is a far cry from the place Abigail Adams used many years ago to hang out her laundry.

The Green Room

Although it was originally planned as a dining room, today the Green Room is a parlor. Its walls are covered with moss-green watered-silk, and it looks much as it did in the early 19th century. The Green Room could be called a Federal parlor in a traditional classic style. Furnished with pieces from the Jeffersonian era, the Green Room was the favorite room of President John F. Kennedy.

The Blue Room

The walls of this formal reception room are hung in a cream-striped satin, but the color blue is in the hangings, the wainscoting and the furniture. The view from the windows of this room shows the south grounds of the White House with the impressive Jefferson Memorial in the background. The color blue is accented with gold in both the draperies and the upholstery used on the furniture.

The Red Room

Still another parlor or sitting room, the walls of the Red Room are hung in cerise silk and the furniture is upholstered in the same. Accents of gold are used here in much the same way as in the Blue Room. The Red Room is a good example of the American Empire period, circa early 1800s.

The State Dining Room

During a formal state dinner, this white and gold room can seat as many as 150 guests. A large well-known portrait of Abraham Lincoln hangs over the fireplace, looking out at the assembled guests. When the table or tables are set for dinner, the array of fine linens, china and silverware, as well as the many crystal wine-glasses, make quite an impressive sight.

The Lincoln Bedroom

Abraham Lincoln used this room as his Cabinet Room. It was here that he signed the Emancipation Proclamation on January 1, 1863 to prohibit slavery in the United States.

Today, this room includes the ornate mahogany bed once used in the state guest chamber. Much of the other furniture in this room came from the Lincoln era in the White House.

The Queen's Bedroom

During the 20th century, queens visiting the United States from Great Britain, the Netherlands and Greece were accommodated in this room. Its decor of red, rose and white offers a pleasant regal setting.

The rooms above are only some which have been used throughout the history of the White House. The contents of each room includes many original pieces as well as excellent copies of period pieces. The china collection, the furniture and the many great paintings throughout the mansion are all worthy of individual study in themselves. A visit to the nation's capital cannot be called complete unless it includes a visit to the President's home — The White House.

Declaration of Independence

When in the Course of human events, it becomes necessary for one people to dissolve the political bands which have connected them with another, and to assume among the Powers of the earth, the separate and equal station to which the Laws of Nature and of Nature's God entitle them, a decent respect to the opinions of mankind requires that they should declare the causes which impel them to the separation.

We hold these truths to be self-evident, that all men are created equal, that they are endowed by their Creator with certain unalienable Rights, that among these are Life, Liberty and the pursuit of Happiness. That to secure these rights, Governments are instituted among Men, deriving their just powers from the consent of the governed, That whenever any Form of Government becomes destructive of these ends, it is the Right of the People to alter or to abolish it, and to institute new Government, laying its foundation on such principles and organizing its powers in such form, as to them shall seem most likely to effect their Safety and Happiness. Prudence, indeed, will dictate that Governments long established should not be changed for light and transient causes; and accordingly all experience hath shown, that mankind are more disposed to suffer, while evils are sufferable, than to right themselves by abolishing the forms to which they are accustomed. But when a long train of abuses and usurpations, pursuing invariably the same Object evinces a design to reduce them under absolute Despotism, it is their right, it is their duty, to throw off such Government, and to provide new Guards for their future security.—Such has been the patient sufferance of these Colonies; and such is now the necessity which constrains them to alter their former Systems of Government. The history of the present King of Great Britain is a history of repeated injuries and usurpations, all having in direct object the establishment of an absolute Tyranny over these States. To prove this, let Facts be submitted to a candid world.

He has refused his Assent to Laws, the most wholesome and necessary for the public good.

He has forbidden his Governors to pass Laws of immediate and pressing importance, unless suspended in their operation till his Assent should be obtained; and when so suspended, he has utterly neglected to attend to them.

He has refused to pass other Laws for the accommodation of large districts of people, unless those people would relinquish the right of Representation in the Legislature, a right inestimable to them and formidable to tyrants only.

He has called together legislative bodies at places unusual, uncomfortable, and distant from the depository of their Public Records, for the sole purpose of fatiguing them into compliance with his measures.

He has dissolved Representative Houses repeatedly, for opposing with manly firmness his invasions on the rights of the people.

He has refused for a long time, after such dissolutions, to cause others to be elected; whereby the Legislative Powers, incapable of Annihilation, have returned to the People at large for their exercise; the State remaining in the mean time exposed to all the dangers of invasion from without, and convulsions within.

He has endeavoured to prevent the population of these States; for that purpose obstructing the Laws for Naturalization of Foreigners; refusing to pass others to encourage their migrations hither, and raising the conditions of new Appropriations of Lands.

He has obstructed the Administration of Justice, by refusing his Assent to Laws for establishing Judiciary Powers.

He has made Judges dependent on his Will alone, for the tenure of their offices, and the amount and payment of their salaries.

He has erected a multitude of New Offices, and sent hither swarms of Officers to harass our people, and eat out their substance.

He has kept among us, in times of peace, Standing Armies without the Consent of our legislatures.

He has affected to render the Military independent of and superior to the Civil Power.

He has combined with others to subject us to a jurisdiction foreign to our constitution, and unacknowledged by our laws; giving his Assent to their acts of pretended Legislation:

For quartering large bodies of armed troops among us:

For protecting them, by a mock Trial, from Punishment for any Murders which they should commit on the Inhabitants of these States:

For cutting off our Trade with all parts of the world:

For imposing taxes on us without our Consent:

For depriving us in many cases, of the benefits of Trial by Jury:

For transporting us beyond Seas to be tried for pretended offences:

For abolishing the free System of English Laws in a neighbouring Province, establishing therein an Arbitrary government, and enlarging its Boundaries so as to render it at once an example and fit instrument for introducing the same absolute rule into these Colonies:

For taking away our Charters, abolishing our most valuable Laws, and altering fundamentally the Forms of our Governments:

For suspending our own Legislatures, and declaring themselves invested with power to legislate for us in all cases whatsoever.

He has abdicated Government here, by declaring us out of his Protection and waging War against us.

He has plundered our seas, ravaged our Coasts, burnt our towns, and destroyed the lives of our people.

He is at this time transporting large armies of foreign mercenaries to compleat the works of death, desolation and tyranny, already begun with circumstances of Cruelty & perfidy scarcely paralleled in the most barbarous ages, and totally unworthy the Head of a civilized nation.

He has constrained our fellow Citizens taken Captive on the high Seas to bear Arms against their Country, to become the executioners of their friends and Brethren, or to fall themselves by their Hands.

He has excited domestic insurrections amongst us, and has endeavoured to bring on the inhabitants of our frontiers, the merciless Indian Savages, whose known rule of warfare, is an undistinguished destruction of all ages, sexes and conditions.

In every stage of these Oppressions We have Petitioned for Redress in the most humble terms: Our repeated Petitions have been answered only by repeated injury. A Prince whose character is thus marked by every act which may define a Tyrant, is unfit to be the ruler of a free people.

Nor have We been wanting in attentions to our Brittish brethren. We have warned them from time to time of attempts by their legislature to extend an unwarrantable jurisdiction over us. We have reminded them of the circumstances of our emigration and settlement here. We have appealed to their native justice and magnanimity, and we have conjured them by the ties of our common kindred to disavow these usurpations which, would inevitably interrupt our connections and correspondence. They too have been deaf to the voice of justice and of consanguinity. We must, therefore, acquiesce in the necessity, which denounces our Separation, and hold them, as we hold the rest of mankind, Enemies in War, in Peace Friends.

We, therefore, the Representatives of the united States of America, in General Congress, Assembled, appealing to the Supreme Judge of the world for the rectitude of our intentions, do, in the Name, and by authority of the good People of these Colonies, solemnly publish and declare, That these United Colonies are, and of Right ought to be Free and Independent States; that they are Absolved from all Allegiance to the British Crown, and that all political connection between them and the State of Great Britain, is and ought to be totally dissolved; and that as Free and Independent States, they have full power to levy War, conclude Peace, contract Alliances, establish Commerce, and to do all other Acts and Things which Independent States may of right do. And for the support of this Declaration, with a firm reliance on the Protection of Divine Providence, we mutually pledge to each other our Lives, our Fortunes and our sacred Honor.

INDEX GUIDE TO THE CONSTITUTION OF THE UNITED STATES

Preamble.

ARTICLE 1.—The Legislative Department consisting of a Senate and a House of Representatives.
Organization of Congress and terms, qualifications, apportionment and elections.
Impeachment procedures.
Privileges and compensation.
Lawmaking procedures.
Congressional powers.
Limitations on the States and Congress.

ARTICLE II.—The Executive Department.
Election of the President and the Vice-President.
Presidential duties and powers.
Ratification of treaties.
Impeachment of officers.

ARTICLE III.—The Judiciary Department.
Judicial independence.
Jurisdiction of the courts.
Trial by jury guaranteed.
Definition of treason and punishment.

ARTICLE IV.—Position of States and territories.
Full faith and credit to public acts and the judicial proceedings.
Privileges and immunities of citizens of each state.
Fugitives from justice.
Congressional control over territories.
Guarantees and protection to the States.

ARTICLE V.—Methods of amending the Constitution.

ARTICLE VI.—Supremacy of the Constitution, treaties and laws. Oath of Office.

ARTICLE VII.—Method of ratification of the Constitution.

CONSTITUTIONAL AMENDMENTS

Original Ten-Bill of Rights

1. Freedom of religion, speech, press and assembly. Right to petition.
2. Right to keep and bear arms.
3. Quartering of soldiers.
4. Protection from unreasonable search and seizure.
5. Due process in criminal cases. Limitation on right of eminent domain.
6. Right to speedy trial, witnesses and counsel.
7. Right of trial by jury.
8. Excessive bail and cruel punishment forbidden.
9. Retention of rights of the people.
10. Undelegated powers belong to the States or to the people.
11. States exempted from suits by individuals.
12. New method of selecting the President and Vice-President.
13. Abolition of slavery.
14. Definition of citizenship. Guarantees of due process and protection against state action. Apportionment of Congressional Representatives. Certain public debts held valid.
15. Equal rights to vote for white and black citizens.
16. Authorization of income tax.
17. Popular election of Senators.
18. Prohibition of intoxicating liquors.
19. Extension of suffrage to women.
20. Change in presidential and congressional terms.
21. Repeal of the Eighteenth Amendment.
22. Limitation of President's term in office to two four-year terms.
23. Extension of suffrage to District of Columbia in presidential elections.
24. Poll tax barred in Federal Elections.
25. Succession of the Vice-President to Presidency; fill the office of Vice-President.
26. Lowering voting age to 18 years.

ENTRY OF STATES INTO THE UNION

State	Capital	Entered Union	State	Capital	Entered Union
1. Alabama	Montgomery	1819	26. Montana	Helena	1889
2. Alaska	Juneau	1958	27. Nebraska	Lincoln	1867
3. Arizona	Phoenix	1912	28. Nevada	Carson City	1864
4. Arkansas	Little Rock	1836	*29. New Hampshire	Concord	1788
5. California	Sacramento	1850	*30. New Jersey	Trenton	1787
6. Colorado	Denver	1876	31. New Mexico	Santa Fe	1912
*7. Connecticut	Hartford	1788	*32. New York	Albany	1788
*8. Delaware	Dover	1787	*33. North Carolina	Raleigh	1789
9. Florida	Tallahassee	1845	34. North Dakota	Bismarck	1889
*10. Georgia	Atlanta	1788	35. Ohio	Columbus	1803
11. Hawaii	Honolulu	1959	36. Oklahoma	Oklahoma City	1907
12. Idaho	Boise	1890	37. Oregon	Salem	1859
13. Illinois	Springfield	1818	*38. Pennsylvania	Harrisburg	1787
14. Indiana	Indianapolis	1816	*39. Rhode Island	Providence	1790
15. Iowa	Des Moines	1846	*40. South Carolina	Columbia	1788
16. Kansas	Topeka	1861	41. South Dakota	Pierre	1889
17. Kentucky	Frankfort	1792	42. Tennessee	Nashville	1796
18. Louisiana	Baton Rouge	1812	43. Texas	Austin	1845
19. Maine	Augusta	1820	44. Utah	Salt Lake City	1896
*20. Maryland	Annapolis	1788	45. Vermont	Montpelier	1791
*21. Massachusetts	Boston	1788	*46. Virginia	Richmond	1788
22. Michigan	Lansing	1837	47. Washington	Olympia	1889
23. Minnesota	St. Paul	1858	48. West Virginia	Charleston	1863
24. Mississippi	Jackson	1817	49. Wisconsin	Madison	1848
25. Missouri	Jefferson City	1821	50. Wyoming	Cheyenne	1890

*Thirteen Original States to Ratify the Constitution.